BEFORE WE WERE BORN

The Sacred Stages of the Soul Before Incarnation

VOLUME I

Nothing is random. You chose this life—now remember why.

SHREE SHAMBAV

AF530191

BEFORE WE WERE BORN
The Sacred Stages of the Soul Before Incarnation
Volume One

Shree Shambav

Published by Shree Shambav, Tamil Nadu, India
Shree Shambav Ink & Imagination "Where Words Breathe and Imagination Soars"

First Edition, 2026

ISBN: 978-93-5692-054-5
Email:shreeshambav@gmail.com
Web:www.shambav.org

DEDICATION

"Isavasyam idam sarvam yat kim ca jagatyam jagat, tena tyaktena bhunjitha, ma gridhah kasyasvid dhanam"

To the Almighty,

the Divine Masters,

the family who listens,

and my parents who see –

your presence shapes the pages of my life's journey.

"Isavasyam idam sarvam yat kim ca jagatyam jagat"

Meaning: "God encompasses everything you perceive, see, or touch with your sense organs."

DISCLAIMER

Before We Were Born is a contemplative and philosophical exploration of spiritual ideas concerning the nature of the soul, consciousness, and the stages believed to precede human incarnation. This work arises from the author's sincere inquiry into ancient wisdom traditions, personal reflection, and symbolic understanding of existence. It is offered as a meditative invitation, not as an assertion of absolute truth.

The content of this book is intended solely for personal reflection, spiritual contemplation, and educational enrichment. It represents interpretive insights drawn from spiritual texts, cross-cultural philosophies, and inner inquiry, and should not be understood as scientific fact, religious doctrine, or professional guidance of any kind. Nothing within these pages is intended to replace medical, psychological, legal, financial, or therapeutic advice from qualified professionals.

While care has been taken to present ideas with integrity and depth, the author makes no guarantees regarding accuracy, universality, or applicability to individual belief systems or life circumstances. By engaging with this book, readers acknowledge that any interpretations, emotional responses, or personal reflections that arise are their own responsibility. The author shall not be held liable for any direct or indirect effects resulting from the use or understanding of the material presented.

Explorations of the soul, memory, and consciousness may evoke introspection, emotional sensitivity, or shifts in perspective. Such responses are natural aspects of inner inquiry and are intended to encourage awareness, not distress. Readers are encouraged to approach the material with discernment, balance, and self-compassion.

This book does not seek to persuade, convert, or define belief. It does not claim authority over spiritual truth, but rather invites a quiet dialogue with timeless questions of existence. It is a symbolic map, not a destination—an offering meant to inspire reflection, not certainty.

Ultimately, *Before We Were Born* is shared in humility and reverence, trusting the reader's wisdom to integrate what resonates and release what does not.

Note: For knowledge and contemplative purposes only.

Note - If any part of the book, in any sequence, hurts the reader's sentiments, it would be just out of a sheer accident not intentional

EPIGRAPH

Before the body learned to breathe,

the soul learned to choose.

Before time began counting,

consciousness was already waiting—

not to enter life,

but to remember itself through it.

– Shree Shambav

BEFORE WE WERE BORN

The Sacred Stages of the Soul Before Incarnation

Nothing is random. You chose this life—now remember why.

SHREE SHAMBAV

Shree Shambav is a 118x best-selling author, renowned for his transformative works in personal development and spiritual growth

Dear Cherished Readers

Dear Cherished Readers,

As I embark on this new literary voyage, my heart swells with profound gratitude and an overwhelming sense of connection. With deep emotion, I extend my heartfelt appreciation to each of you who has joined me on this journey.

With sincere warmth, I invite you to revisit the steps we have taken together through the pages of my earlier works. Our odyssey began with "Journey of Soul - Karma," a book that marked my first foray into the world of words and a testament to the raw passion that ignited my writing adventure.

The subsequent chapters of our shared journey unfolded through the enchanting tapestry of the *"Twenty + One"* series. With each page turned, it felt as though a brushstroke was added to the canvas of our collective imagination—stories and sentiments woven to echo within the quiet corners of your heart. These weren't just words; they were invitations to feel, to reflect, and to remember what truly matters.

And how can I not cherish the transformative path we walked together through the *"Life Changing Journey—Inspirational Quotes Series?"* Day by day, quote by quote, we ventured inward—into spaces often overlooked—to find wisdom in simplicity and light in life's shadows. Each reflection was offered as a gentle whisper of hope, a spark meant to uplift, inspire, and remind us that even in silence, the soul speaks.

The release of "Death - Light of Life and the Shadow of Death" promises to shed new light on the timeless mystery of death.

The **Optimum Python Series** is a comprehensive learning pathway designed to empower readers at every stage of their programming journey. It begins with **Series I: Ultimate Guide for Beginners**, which builds a strong and accessible foundation in Python for newcomers. **Series II: Exploring Data Structures and Algorithms** advances into core computer science concepts, strengthening problem-solving skills and coding efficiency.

Building on this, **Series III: Python Power for Data Science** introduces powerful libraries such as NumPy, Pandas, Matplotlib, and Scikit-learn, guiding readers through data manipulation, visualisation, and foundational machine learning techniques. **Series IV:**

Unleashing the Potential of Data Science with Machine Learning Techniques explores advanced models and real-world applications.

This progression continues with **Series V: Optimum: Python Power – Unleashing the Potential of Data Science with Deep Learning Techniques**, and culminates in **Series VI: From Data to Intelligence – The Deep Learning Revolution**, enabling readers to harness the full potential of data-driven innovation. Whether you are a beginner or an advanced learner, this series serves as your complete roadmap to Python mastery and beyond.

Shree Shambav expands his artistic repertoire with *Whispers of Eternity: A Symphony of Soulful Verses*, a heartfelt exploration of the human experience expressed through lyrical depth and timeless reflection. Complementing this, his *Whispers of the Soul: A Journey Through Haiku* distils profound truths into delicate, poignant verses, capturing the fleeting essence of life with elegant simplicity.

Equally evocative, *Whispers of Stillness: Where the Soul Listens Beyond the Noise* offers meditative couplets that invite readers into silence, where wisdom blossoms in the spaces between words. Together, these works illuminate Shambav's versatility and mastery of soulful expression. They invite readers on a transformative journey of self-discovery, weaving a tapestry of emotion, insight, and transcendence that lingers long after the final page is turned.

Building on this success, he continued to enchant audiences with his subsequent albums: HeartStrings, *Melodies of the Heart*, *Driftwood Memories*, *Winds of Change, The Veil and the Waves, Echoes of the Soul, Phoenix Within,* Uncaged, Where Nature Sings, and Wings of Forever. Each album further solidified his place in the world of music, offering a mesmerising collection of tracks that evoke nostalgia, introspection, and heartfelt connection. With every composition, Shree Shambav weaves a musical journey that lingers in the soul long after the final note fades.

Shree Shambav's latest works shine as luminous beacons on the path of self-discovery, mindful living, and spiritual awakening. His writings span a vast spectrum of human experience, each book offering a doorway to transformation. Among his most celebrated titles are Learn to Love Yourself: A Journey of Discovering Inner Beauty and Strength Through 10 Transformative Rules, The Power of Letting Go: Embrace Freedom and Happiness, A Journey of Lasting Peace, and The Entitlement Trap: Get Over It, Get On.

His thought-provoking works include Whispers of a Dying Soul: Unspoken Regrets and Unlived Dreams, Whispers of Silence: Unlocking Inner Power through Stillness, The Power of Words: Transforming Speech,

Transforming Lives, The Art of Intentional Living: Minimalism for a Life of Purpose, and Awakening the Infinite: The Power of Consciousness in Transforming Life.

In The Power of Manifestation: Unlocking the Path from Thought to Reality, Shree Shambav presents a transformative roadmap for turning vision into lived experience, guiding readers from intention to realisation. Beyond the Veil: A Journey Through Life After Death ventures into the profound mystery of existence beyond the physical realm, inviting contemplation on life, transition, and the eternal soul.

His other compelling works include Bonds Beyond Blood: Where Love Builds Bridges and Bonds Defy Lineage, a heartfelt celebration of love that transcends ancestry and form; The Inner Battlefield: Overcoming the Enemies of the Mind and Soul, a powerful guide to mastering inner conflicts and reclaiming mental sovereignty; and A Journey into Spiritual Maturity: 12 Golden Rules for Inner Transformation, which offers timeless wisdom for seekers evolving toward self-mastery and inner awakening.

In The Seeker's Gold: Unlocking Life's Greatest Treasure, he inspires readers to uncover the hidden riches of the soul, while The Law of Attraction: A Soulful Path reveals how to harmonise thought, energy, and intention to create a life aligned with one's highest purpose. His transformative Born to Rise series further empowers readers to embrace growth, clarity, and lasting fulfilment across every dimension of life.

Shree Shambav is also the author of Mastering the Art of Gratitude: A Journey from Acknowledgement to Awakening, a contemplative series on conscious appreciation, and Whispers of a Silent Monk: Poetic Tales of Love, Loss, and Liberation, a lyrical exploration of silence, surrender, and inner freedom.

In addition, his works Journey of the Soul – Karma Unveiled, Unveiling the Enigma, and Death: Light of Life and the Shadow of Death have been translated into Gujarati and Hindi, extending his spiritual insights to a wider audience.

In addition to these works, Shree Shambav has recently ventured into astrology with the release of Astrology Unveiled – Foundations of Ancient Wisdom Series I to XIX, expanding into the realm of metaphysics. These books explore the foundational principles of Vedic astrology, offering readers a rich and practical understanding of this ancient wisdom.

Your unwavering support, enthusiasm to immerse yourself in my writings, and readiness to embark on these journeys with me have been my greatest sources of inspiration. Your input has been a beacon guiding me through the creation process, moulding these stories into containers of passion, emotion, knowledge, and resonance.

As I unveil this new narrative before you, know that your presence, insights, and shared moments have been my companions. The path we have walked together is etched in the annals of my creative evolution, and it's an honour beyond words to have you by my side once more.

Here's to the readers who have illuminated my path with their presence, who have embraced my stories with open hearts, and who have woven themselves into the very fabric of my literary world. Our journey has been a symbiotic dance of writer and reader, a harmony of souls brought together by the magic of storytelling.

With a heart brimming with appreciation and eyes glistening with anticipation, I extend my deepest gratitude for your unwavering support. Thank you for the memories, the shared emotions, and the countless hours spent in the worlds we've crafted together. As we step into this new adventure, let's continue to explore, feel, and discover the boundless horizons that words can unveil.

Warmly,

Shree Shambav

Suggested Reads

FROM BEST SELLING AUTHOR

ENDORSEMENTS

A profound and luminous work, Before We Were Born invites readers into the sacred architecture of existence itself. Blending ancient wisdom with poetic clarity, the book does not demand belief—it awakens remembrance. Each chapter feels like a quiet conversation with eternity, offering depth without dogma and insight without fear. This is not a book to be rushed, but one to be lived with. It gently reshapes how we understand birth, purpose, pain, and the unseen intelligence guiding every life.

— Roopa

About the Author

Shree Shambav is an internationally acclaimed best-selling author, inspirational speaker, artist, philanthropist, life coach, strategist, and entrepreneur. A world record holder, his deep passion for music led him to create soul-stirring albums, drawing inspiration from his celebrated poetry collection, Whispers of Eternity. His profound insights have sparked deep personal transformations, guiding countless individuals toward self-discovery, purposeful living, and authenticity.

With an extraordinary ability to unlock human potential, Shree empowers individuals to break through limitations and embrace their highest selves. His writings, lectures, and compassionate guidance continue to uplift lives, fostering resilience, mindfulness, and personal growth.

Shree Shambav is a 118x best-selling author celebrated for his profound contributions to personal development and spiritual growth.

Shree Shambav's literary journey took flight with the celebrated Journey of Soul - Karma, where he delved into the depths of human experience to unveil profound insights. Garnering recognition through multiple literature awards, his repertoire includes esteemed works, such as the Twenty + One Series, and the enlightening Life Changing Journey – Inspirational Quotes series.

As a distinguished alumnus of the Indian Institute of Management and the National Institute of Technology, Shree Shambav brings a wealth of corporate acumen from his tenure in multinational corporations. His most recent publications, including Unveiling the Enigma, Death - Light of Life and the Shadow of Death, and Optimum – Power Python Series I, Series II, Series III, Series IV, Series V, and Series VI, demonstrate his mastery of both the literary and technical spheres.

Shree Shambav expands his artistic repertoire with *Whispers of Eternity: A Symphony of Soulful Verses*, a heartfelt exploration of the human experience expressed through lyrical depth and timeless reflection. Complementing this, his *Whispers of the Soul: A Journey Through Haiku* distils profound truths into delicate, poignant verses, capturing the fleeting essence of life with elegant simplicity.

Equally evocative, *Whispers of Stillness: Where the Soul Listens Beyond the Noise* offers meditative couplets that invite readers into silence, where wisdom blossoms in the spaces between words. Together, these works illuminate Shambav's versatility and mastery of soulful expression. They invite readers on a transformative journey of self-discovery, weaving a tapestry of emotion, insight, and transcendence that lingers long after the final page is turned.

Building on this success, he continued to enchant audiences with his subsequent albums: HeartStrings, *Melodies of the Heart*, *Driftwood Memories*, *Winds of Change, The Veil and the Waves, Echoes of the Soul, Phoenix Within,* Uncaged, Where Nature Sings, and Wings of Forever. Each album further solidified his place in the world of music, offering a mesmerising collection of tracks that evoke nostalgia, introspection, and heartfelt connection. With every composition, Shree Shambav weaves a musical journey that lingers in the soul long after the final note fades.

Shree Shambav's latest works shine as luminous beacons on the path of self-discovery, mindful living, and spiritual awakening. His writings span a vast spectrum of human experience, each book offering a doorway to transformation. Among his most celebrated titles are Learn to Love Yourself: A Journey of Discovering Inner Beauty and Strength Through 10 Transformative Rules, The Power of Letting Go: Embrace Freedom and Happiness, A Journey of Lasting Peace, and The Entitlement Trap: Get Over It, Get On.

His thought-provoking works include Whispers of a Dying Soul: Unspoken Regrets and Unlived Dreams, Whispers of Silence: Unlocking Inner Power through Stillness, The Power of Words: Transforming Speech, Transforming Lives, The Art of Intentional Living: Minimalism for a Life of Purpose, and Awakening the Infinite: The Power of Consciousness in Transforming Life.

In The Power of Manifestation: Unlocking the Path from Thought to Reality, Shree Shambav presents a transformative roadmap for turning vision into lived experience, guiding readers from intention to realisation. Beyond the Veil: A Journey Through Life After Death ventures into the profound mystery of existence beyond the physical realm, inviting contemplation on life, transition, and the eternal soul.

His other compelling works include Bonds Beyond Blood: Where Love Builds Bridges and Bonds Defy Lineage, a heartfelt celebration of love that transcends ancestry and form; The Inner Battlefield: Overcoming the Enemies of the Mind and Soul, a powerful guide to mastering inner conflicts and reclaiming mental sovereignty; and A Journey into Spiritual Maturity: 12 Golden Rules for Inner Transformation, which offers timeless wisdom for seekers evolving toward self-mastery and inner awakening.

In The Seeker's Gold: Unlocking Life's Greatest Treasure, he inspires readers to uncover the hidden riches of the soul, while The Law of Attraction: A Soulful Path reveals how to harmonise thought, energy, and intention to create a life aligned with one's highest purpose. His transformative Born to Rise series further empowers readers to embrace growth, clarity, and lasting fulfilment across every dimension of life.

Shree Shambav is also the author of Mastering the Art of Gratitude: A Journey from Acknowledgement to Awakening, a contemplative series on conscious appreciation, and Whispers of a Silent Monk: Poetic Tales of Love, Loss, and Liberation, a lyrical exploration of silence, surrender, and inner freedom.

In addition, his works Journey of the Soul – Karma Unveiled, Unveiling the Enigma, and Death: Light of Life and the Shadow of Death have been translated into Gujarati and Hindi, extending his spiritual insights to a wider audience.

In addition to these works, Shree Shambav has recently ventured into astrology with the release of Astrology Unveiled – Foundations of Ancient Wisdom Series I to XVII, expanding into the realm of metaphysics. These books explore the foundational principles of Vedic astrology, offering readers a rich and practical understanding of this ancient wisdom.

Shree Shambav established the Ayur Rakshita Foundation, which is dedicated to promoting boundless growth, universal fraternity, and environmental protection. The charity helps diverse communities while working for societal progress.

To learn more about Shree Shambav and his works, visit his website at www.shambav.org. For information about the Ayur Rakshita Foundation and its initiatives, visit www.shambav-ayurrakshita.org.

Let's Follow him on Social Media: **@shreeshambav**

Main: https://linktr.ee/shreeshambav

PREFACE

This book was not written to explain life—it was written to listen to it.

For years, questions surfaced again and again in conversations, silences, teachings, and tears: *Why this life? Why this body? Why these patterns that repeat even when we try to escape them?* Beneath every spiritual practice, philosophical inquiry, and moment of suffering lay a quieter question still—*Was this chosen, or merely endured?*

Before We Were Born emerged from that listening.

It does not claim final answers, nor does it ask for belief. Instead, it offers a contemplative map—drawn not from imagination alone, but from the shared wisdom of seekers across ages and traditions. The Bhagavad Gita, the Upanishads, the Puranas, the Bible, Sufi poetry, and other mystical streams are not treated here as separate authorities, but as different languages pointing toward the same interior truth: that consciousness is older than birth, and intention deeper than circumstance.

This book was written slowly, in pauses between words, in the spaces where teaching becomes transmission. Many of its insights arose not from study, but from stillness—moments when questions dissolved, and understanding arrived without explanation. What you will find here is not doctrine, but orientation. Not a system to adopt, but a way of seeing.

The central premise may feel unsettling at first: that the soul participates in its own becoming. That life is not imposed from above nor random from below, but consciously entered. This does not deny pain, injustice, or suffering. On the contrary, it takes them seriously—seriously enough to ask *why an eternal intelligence would willingly pass through limitation, forgetting, and struggle.*

To ask that question honestly is to move beyond blame—of fate, of divine, of oneself—and toward responsibility rooted in compassion. Responsibility is not a burden, but an awakening.

Throughout these pages, you will encounter stories rather than arguments, metaphors rather than mandates. A flame that longs to illuminate form. A river of light where memory becomes feeling. Councils of guidance that do not command but remind. These are not meant to be taken literally, nor dismissed symbolically. They are mirrors—reflecting truths that each reader must recognise in their own way.

If at times the writing feels intimate, that is intentional. These teachings were never meant to remain abstract. They speak to grief that has no language, to longing that survives fulfilment, to the strange familiarity of moments that feel remembered rather than learned.

You may read this book as philosophy. You may read it as spiritual psychology. Or you may read it as a quiet companion during a season of inner questioning. Read it slowly. Let certain passages rest with you. Disagreement is welcome. Reflection is essential.

This is Part One of a larger journey. It speaks of what precedes birth—not to escape life, but to enter it more consciously. The remaining stages and deeper truths will unfold in Part Two, where the soul's descent into form and its return toward remembrance are explored further.

If this book succeeds, it will not be because it convinces you of something new. It will be because it helps you remember something old.

Something you may have known

before you were born.

With kindest regards,

Shree Shambav

CONTENTS

INTRODUCTION

There is a question that visits every human life, often in moments of quiet rather than crisis:

Why am I here?

Not merely here in this place or this time—but here at all. Why this body, this temperament, this family, this set of longings and limitations? Why does something within us remember more than we seem to know?

Before We Were Born begins with this silent inquiry.

This book does not attempt to prove the soul as an object, nor does it offer belief as consolation. Instead, it invites the reader into a deeper listening—toward what has always been sensed but rarely named. Across cultures and centuries, mystics, sages, and seekers have spoken of a truth that precedes birth: that existence is not accidental, and that consciousness does not begin with the body nor end with it.

At the heart of this work lies a simple yet radical premise: **the soul does not rush into life—it prepares for it.**

Part One, **The Eternal Architect**, explores what exists before identity takes form. It asks what the soul is when it is not defined by name, memory, or role. Here, the soul is revealed as timeless awareness—complete, luminous, yet moved by a quiet urge to experience itself through relationship, resistance, and reflection. Birth is not portrayed as a fall into limitation, but as a sacred choice: fullness seeking expression.

Through contemplative analogies, lived stories, and insights drawn from ancient philosophies, the chapters examine the invisible structures that support life—prana as the animating force, consciousness as the field of experience, and the Akashic Field as the subtle memory of all that has ever been lived. Karma is reframed not as reward or punishment, but as precise intelligence—an elegant mathematics of cause, consequence, and understanding.

Part Two, **The Sacred Preparation**, moves closer to the threshold of incarnation. It reveals the stages through which the soul passes before entering a new life: the call of universal consciousness, the profound reckoning of the life review, and the compassionate collaboration of the Councils of the Soul. These are not realms of judgment, but of clarity—where understanding replaces guilt, and choice replaces compulsion.

Throughout the book, wisdom from the Bhagavad Gita, Upanishads, Puranas, Biblical teachings, Sufi mysticism, and other spiritual traditions is woven seamlessly into lived insight—not as doctrine, but as echoes of a shared remembrance. These traditions are treated not as authorities to obey, but as companions pointing toward the same horizon.

This is not a book meant to be rushed. It is meant to be entered slowly, as one enters a sacred space. Some passages may feel like recognition rather than revelation. Others may unsettle long-held assumptions. That, too, is part of the preparation.

If you have ever felt a restlessness that success could not silence, a longing that had no clear object, or a sense that your life carries a deeper intention than circumstances suggest—this book is for you.

It does not promise answers that close the mystery.

It invites awareness that opens it.

For before we were born, something chose to be known.

And that choosing, quietly, continues through you.

Warm regards,

Shree Shambav

PROLOGUE

Before Memory, Before Name

Before breath learned its rhythm
before the body claimed its shape
before the world spoke to you in language and
form—
there was awareness.

Not awareness *of* something,
but awareness *itself.*

No edges. No centre.
No beginning asking for an end.

And yet—something stirred.

Not hunger.
Not need.
Not lack.

A subtle leaning.

Like light turning toward reflection.
Like silence sensing the possibility of song.

Long before birth, before ancestry and circumstance, there was a pause in eternity—a moment so still that even timelessness became aware of itself. In that stillness, nothing was missing. And yet, something was calling—not from outside, but from within fullness itself.

The soul did not fall into life.
It inclined toward it.

Across civilisations and centuries, mystics have tried to name this moment. The Upanishads whisper, *"Let me enter into forms."* The Gita speaks of the Eternal choosing to move within nature. Sufi poets say the Beloved hid so that love could seek. The Gospel tells of the Word becoming flesh—not out of weakness, but out of love for closeness.

Different languages.
One gesture.

To experience.
To remember through forgetting.
To know wholeness by touching limitation.

What we call *life* begins there.

Not as punishment.
Not an accident.
Not as debt.

But as consent.

This book begins before the first cry, before the first wound, before the first triumph. It begins where choice is quieter than thought and intention moves without words. It explores what may have happened before you were given a name—when awareness prepared itself to wear time, relationship, and story.

If you have ever felt a restlessness that success could not settle,
a longing that love could not exhaust,
a sense that you are living something remembered rather than learned—
this book is speaking to that place.

You do not need to believe its images.
You only need to listen for resonance.

Because some truths are not recognised by agreement,
but by familiarity.

And perhaps, as you turn these pages,
something in you will not feel informed—
but remembered.

As if a quiet voice within says,

Yes. This was known.

Warm regards,

Shree Shambav

Prelude

The Silence Before the First Question

There is a silence that exists before every beginning.

Not the silence that follows sound, but the silence that gives birth to it.

Before a question rises, before curiosity takes shape, there is a quiet awareness that senses mystery without needing to solve it. This book is born in that silence—not to explain life as a problem, but to approach existence as a sacred unfolding.

Long before we ask *Who am I?* or *Why am I here?*, something within us already knows it is here **on purpose**. This knowing is not logical; it is intuitive, ancient, and strangely intimate. It appears in childhood wonder, in moments of awe, in grief that feels larger than circumstance, and in love that seems to remember us more than we remember it.

The modern world trains us to look outward—toward achievements, identities, and answers that can be measured. Yet across traditions, from rishis to mystics, from desert hermits to Himalayan sages, one insight repeats quietly: **life does not begin at birth, and the self does not end at death.**

Between those two illusions stretches a vast preparation.

This prelude is not an argument.

It is an invitation.

An invitation to loosen the grip of certainty and allow mystery to breathe again. To read not with the mind alone, but with the subtle intelligence of the heart—the place that recognises truth before it is proven.

The chapters that follow will speak of the soul, of consciousness, of karmic design and cosmic order. They will explore the possibility that existence is not random, but patterned; not chaotic, but deeply intentional. Yet these ideas are offered not as doctrine, but as mirrors—ways of seeing that may help you glimpse your own deeper continuity.

If at times the language feels poetic rather than precise, it is because some realities dissolve when handled too tightly. If certain passages awaken discomfort or wonder, allow them to. Growth often begins where familiarity ends.

This book does not ask you to escape the world. It asks you to understand why you entered it.

And so, before we speak of souls choosing lives, before councils and cosmic laws are named, we pause here—at the threshold. Where nothing has yet begun, and everything is already present.

Take this moment slowly.

For what you are about to read is not merely about *before you were born.*

It is about the part of you that has never left.

At Kanchipuram

"You were not placed into this life by chance; you stepped into it with courage. Every breath you take is an echo of a 'yes' you once spoke in full awareness."

- *Shree Shambav.*

Even before the sun remembered how to rise, during Brahma Muhurtam, the world around Kanchipuram rested in a sacred hush—like a temple holding its breath before the first bell. Darkness still lingered, but it was no longer heavy; it had softened into a velvety blue, as though night itself was bowing in reverence to the coming light.

Beneath the ancient banyan tree—its roots hanging like the matted locks of a silent sage—Akshaya and Vasudeva sat cross-legged upon the cool earth. The ground felt alive, gently pulsing, as if the soil itself was meditating with them. Without words, without signal, their eyes closed, spines aligned, breaths settling into a rhythm older than language. The banyan did not merely shade them; it witnessed them, as it had witnessed centuries of seekers before.

Moments later, Kiran arrived, his footsteps careful, as though not to disturb the silence but to merge into it. Vidyarthi followed, carrying the calm of someone who had already arrived inwardly long before arriving here. They joined the circle without greeting, without gesture—because at that hour, even names felt unnecessary. Four breaths, four bodies, one stillness.

Time loosened its grip.

An hour passed—not measured by clocks, but by the softening of effort, by the moment when thought thinned and presence deepened. When their eyes finally opened, there was no dramatic movement, no sudden awakening. Instead, their faces carried a quiet luminosity—the subtle glow of inner waters finally becoming still. It was not happiness, not bliss, but something truer: resting in oneself.

Their morning walk followed, not as exercise, but as prayer in motion. Each step was unhurried, deliberate, as if the ground beneath their feet were sacred scripture and they were reading it line by line. No one spoke. The silence walked with them like a fifth companion—gentle, intimate, whole.

As they neared the temple grounds, the silence gave way—not abruptly, but like dawn surrendering to music.

The air vibrated with bhajans—tabla and dholak weaving steady heartbeats, the harmonium breathing long, soulful phrases. The sacred syllable Om rose and fell, not chanted but lived, rippling through stone, air, and bone alike. Temple bells rang—not sharp, but round and generous—each peal dissolving into the next, as though time itself were being rung awake.

The fragrance of flowers, sandalwood, and incense drifted freely, curling around pillars, settling into breath, resting briefly on skin before moving on. Holiness was not imposed here; it was ambient, like oxygen.

To one side, devotees moved through yogic postures, bodies stretching toward the sky like quiet prayers written in muscle and breath. Nearby, others tended to the garden, hands in soil, leaves brushed gently aside, every act an offering. No task felt lesser; all work shared the same sanctity.

Morning in Kanchipuram did not arrive like an ordinary day. It unfolded, slowly, reverently—like a forgotten hymn remembered by the soul before the mind could claim it.

A cool breeze slipped through the temple streets, carrying the scent of damp earth and last night's rain, mingled with jasmine's sweetness. Tiny streams murmured beside stone paths, telling stories that had never needed listeners. Leaves held dewdrops like pearls of gratitude. Birds perched in stillness—not yet singing, but preparing, as if awaiting a cue from the cosmos.

In the distance, Aastha, Abhirami, Kiran, Sam, and Alice wandered through Brindavan Garden. Flowers swayed as if responding to an unheard raga, petals bending under the weight of dew—reluctant to release the night, yet eager for the day.

From the temple steps, Akshatha, Nita, Lalitha, Rohith, and Sujitha emerged, their bhajan still echoing softly in their chests, like incense that lingers long after the flame is gone. Soon after, Roopa, Kieron, Astyn, Espen, Greta, and Divyani arrived from their yoga practice, bodies warm, spines open, eyes clear—each carrying the silent alignment that comes when breath and being agree.

This was not a gathering. It was a remembering.

The air itself seemed to whisper, All that you have sought has always been here.

The sun did not rise. It arrived—like an honoured guest, draped in gold, offering its warmth not as command but as blessing. The sky did not blaze; it softened, melting like ghee into a sacred flame. The Earth exhaled, long and contented, as footsteps echoed softly—seekers arriving not at a place, but at a moment.

Sofia, Bhavya, and Akanksh walked the gravel path—not as wanderers, but as pilgrims responding to a call older than memory. Neem leaves rustled overhead, their sound becoming a tanpura drone, tuning the morning itself. Even the banyan trees bowed inwardly, their roots heavy with remembrance, welcoming souls they had known across lifetimes.

Silence accompanied them—not emptiness, but fullness. A silence that listened.

Then Aarna smiled, a small, effortless curve of warmth. “Shall we begin with coffee?” she asked.

The words landed gently, like a bell rung not to awaken the world, but to invite it closer. Cups of steaming coffee and tea appeared in hands, glowing like tiny lamps, warmth travelling from palms to hearts.

Birdsong finally rose—not hurried, not scattered—but slow and devotional, the alaap of the morning raga. Sandalwood mingled with neem blossoms. Laughter flowed softly as Aarna, Dev, and John joined, their presence light, sincere, unforced—sunlight translated into sound.

After a pause that felt complete, Akanksh spoke, his voice steady with reverence. “Guruji will be speaking today about Before We Were Born — The Sacred Stages of the Soul Before Incarnation.”

Nods moved through the circle—not agreement, but readiness.

Then came a deeper hush.

Apeksha lifted her gaze to the banyan canopy, where sunlight filtered through leaves like liquid gold. When her eyes returned to the circle, something subtle had shifted—as if an unseen door had opened quietly within the day itself.

Before she could speak, Abhilasha's voice rose, low and tender, almost a vibration rather than a sound.

"Apeksha," she said softly, "please… tell us a story to begin our day."

Before We Were Born

Apeksha closed her eyes for a moment, not to search for words, but to let them rise. When she spoke, her voice was calm, yet carried a depth that felt older than the banyan tree above them.

"Before we were born," she began softly, "we were not empty. We were not waiting. We were awake."

The group leaned in—not with their bodies, but with something deeper.

"Imagine," she said, "standing at the edge of a vast river of light. Not as a body, not as a name—but as awareness itself. There is no fear there. No urgency. Only clarity. You see your past lives the way you now remember a dream—not with judgment, but with understanding."

She paused. A bird called once, then fell silent.

"You see every moment where you loved fully—and where you held back. You feel the joy you gave others as your own expansion. You feel the pain you caused—not as punishment, but as knowledge. That is how the soul learns. Not through rules, but through experience."

A breeze moved through the circle, as if the banyan itself was listening.

"Then," Apeksha continued, "you are not alone. You never were. Beings of light—guides, masters, companions of many journeys—stand with you. Not above you. With you. Together, you design your next life like an artist choosing colours."

She opened her eyes now, meeting theirs.

"You choose challenges—not because you enjoy suffering, but because you know growth demands friction, just as fire demands wood. You choose parents who will love you imperfectly. A body that will teach you limits. A place on Earth where your lessons will be unavoidable."

Some shifted. Some swallowed.

"You even choose your pain," she said gently. "Because pain is not punishment. Pain is precision. It carves exactly where growth is needed."

She let the words settle.

"And then comes the bravest moment of all—the veil."

Her voice softened further.

"You agree to forget. Not because the truth is dangerous—but because remembering too soon would make the journey meaningless. Forgetting allows sincerity. Struggle becomes real. Choice becomes sacred."

She smiled, faintly.

"That emptiness you feel sometimes? That sense that 'something is missing'? It is not brokenness. It is memory knocking from the inside."

The group was utterly still now.

"You were never thrown into life," Apeksha concluded. "You leapt into it. With courage. With consent. With love."

She looked around the circle.

"And one day—perhaps today, perhaps slowly—you begin to remember. Not the details. But the truth."

Her final words were almost a whisper:

"You are not here by accident. You are here because you once said yes."

Silence followed—not empty, but full.

The banyan leaves rustled. The temple bell rang once in the distance. And somewhere deep within each listener, something ancient stirred—as if a forgotten agreement had just been gently recalled.

Aarna exhaled—a gentle sigh of arrival. "It's time for Guruji's morning session," she said.

The circle settled.

Kanchipuram's sacred rhythm—of breath, bell, bird, and being—now pulsed fully alive within them, ready to listen, ready to remember.

Note: Hereafter, Shree Shambav will be referred to as 'Guruji' means Master.

PART ONE

THE ETERNAL ARCHITECT

Before the soul chooses a life

"The body is not the soul's prison, but its chosen instrument—like a flute shaped so breath may become music."

- *Shree Shambav*

CHAPTER I

What Is the Soul?

"The soul does not seek pleasure or pain; it seeks depth. Experience is the soil in which remembrance takes root."

– Shree Shambav.

Synopsis

This chapter explores the pre-incarnational state of the soul, before birth and before identity forms. It delves into the soul's timeless existence—a vast, unbroken awareness, complete yet stirred by a longing to experience itself through form. Using the analogy of a perfect mirror fracturing to know its own depth, the chapter illustrates that the soul does not enter the body out of incompleteness but to express its fullness and remember its true nature through experience.

Through joy, sorrow, attachment, and release, the soul learns, evolves, and slowly recognises what it never truly forgot. Drawing from texts like the Bhagavad Gita, Nyāya Darśan, and Upanishad philosophy, the chapter bridges classical wisdom with living insight, explaining that birth is never random. Each life, body, family, and circumstance is consciously chosen, a sacred stage in the soul's evolutionary journey, designed for awakening, learning, and alignment with higher consciousness.

All the devotees had settled in Buddha Hall, their eyes calm, their hearts attentive, waiting for their revered Guruji. After a few quiet minutes, Guruji entered, smiling gently and offering Atma Namaskar to each one. He paused for a moment at the centre of the hall, then took his asana with serene grace. Silence settled, soft and expectant.

An Entry into the Journey

Guruji's voice—warm yet commanding—broke the stillness, not as sound but as recognition.

"Before birth becomes breath," he said softly, "before identity learns its name, before memory begins its storytelling, there is a quiet knowing."

He paused, as though listening to something older than language.

"The soul exists in a vast, unbroken awareness—neither beginning nor end, neither inside nor outside. In that state, there is no ambition, no fear, no longing to become anything else. There is no separation. There is only being—complete, luminous, untouched."

It is difficult for the human mind to imagine such fullness, because the mind is born from contrast. Yet the soul is born from wholeness.

"And yet," Guruji continued, "within this completeness arises a subtle stirring. Not a lack. Not dissatisfaction. But a longing of a different order—the longing to experience."

He leaned forward slightly.

"As still water reflects nothing until it is disturbed, consciousness seeks movement to recognise itself. A mirror, flawless and infinite, cannot see its own depth unless something stands before it."

Thus, life is conceived—not as exile from eternity, but as its deliberate expression.

The Story Of The Mirror

Guruji smiled gently and said, "Let me narrate a story."

"An old mystic once spoke of a mirror—perfectly polished, endlessly clear. It reflected mountains and stars, faces and flames, yet it carried a quiet sorrow. Though it revealed everything, it could not see itself."

"One day, out of a desire not born of lack but of curiosity, the mirror fractured into countless shards. Each shard reflected only a fragment of light—an angle, a shadow, a distortion. Some fell into darkness, some into brilliance, some into confusion."

"In those fragments, the mirror learned form and distance, closeness and loss. It learned what it meant to be small, to be partial, to be vulnerable."

"And when the shards were gathered again," Guruji said softly, "the mirror was whole—but now it knew itself."

He looked at Akshaya and said, "So it is with the soul."

The Soul's Descent Into Form

"The soul does not enter the body because it is incomplete," Guruji said. "It enters because completeness longs to be known."

The body becomes its instrument, like a veena tuned for experience. The mind becomes its interface, translating infinity into thought. Life becomes its language, written not in words but in sensations, choices, relationships, and consequences.

"Through joy and sorrow, attachment and release, triumph and grief," Guruji continued, "the soul slowly remembers what it never truly forgot."

After a long pause, he recited:

The Bhagavad Gita reminds us, Chapter 2.22

vasansi jirnani yatha vihaya
navani grihnati naro parani |
tatha sharirani vihaya jirnanya
nyani sanyati navani dehi | |

Then he explained gently:

"As a person discards worn-out garments and wears new ones, the soul discards worn-out bodies and enters new forms. The garment changes—but the wearer remains."

"The soul is not altered by birth or death," Guruji said. "It simply moves, carrying wisdom forward."

Memory, Karma, And The Child's Tears

Guruji then spoke of the newborn child.

"Have you noticed," he asked, "how an infant sometimes smiles without cause, sometimes weeps without reason, sometimes trembles in fear though nothing threatens it?"

"These emotions," he explained, "are echoes—residues of earlier journeys. But as life progresses, the impressions of this world overwrite the older script. Death and birth are powerful crossings; they erase much, but not all."

He continued,

"Consider this also: how does a newborn, without language, seek its mother's milk? Who taught it longing? Who taught it trust?"

"These are not learned," Guruji said. "They are remembered."

Why Inequality Exists

Then his voice grew firmer.

"If life were only one chapter," he said, "then suffering would be cruelty and disparity would be injustice."

"Why is one born into abundance and another into blindness? Why one into love and another into loss?"

"To call it random insults intelligence. To call it divine punishment insults compassion."

"The only explanation that preserves both reason and mercy," Guruji said, "is that the soul chooses experiences—not as punishment, but as preparation."

He looked directly at Akshaya.

"A soul does not fall into life by accident. It chooses—with awareness, preparation, and sacred intention."

The Invitation Ahead

Guruji smiled, his eyes carrying both tenderness and authority.

"Akshaya," he said, "nothing in your life is random. You chose this life—now remember why."

"And this," he said, "is what will unfold: how eternity prepares for form, how consciousness designs experience, and how remembering transforms suffering into wisdom."

The silence that followed was no longer empty. It was alive.

Abhilasha's voice trembled with a mixture of curiosity and reverence. "Guruji," she asked softly, "If the soul is pure witnessing consciousness, eternal and untouched, what is gained—not lost—by entering identity, memory, and form? Why must it descend into limitation to know itself?"

Guruji's eyes are calm yet luminous. "Ah, Abhilasha," he said, "consider the vast sky. It is always limitless, untouched by clouds, storms, or the twilight. Yet, when a river reflects that sky, it is as if the sky experiences itself through ripples, currents, and shadows. The soul, in its eternal state, is like that sky. By entering the form, it becomes the river—flowing, moving, touched by light and shadow. In that reflection, the Self witnesses depth it could never know from stillness alone."

He paused, letting the morning hush settle like incense. "The Bhagavad Gita reminds us: As a man discards worn-out garments and takes on new ones, so too the soul casts aside old bodies to experience anew. Not for loss, but for recognition. Not for suffering, but for expansion."

Guruji continued, voice threaded with warmth, "The Upanishads call it *Atman*—unborn, eternal, undecaying. Yet even the eternal seeks to know itself as many. Like a perfect melody breaking into variations, each note revealing the harmony in a new way, identity, memory, and form allow consciousness to taste the infinite through the finite. The Bible whispers the same truth: the Word became flesh, not to lose divinity, but to manifest it in experience. And the Sufis tell us, the lover must enter the beloved, feel separation, and know reunion, to truly recognise the unity."

Abhilasha's eyes glistened. "So limitation is not imprisonment, but a lens?"

Guruji smiled. "Yes. Each tear, each joy, each fleeting thought is a mirror through which the eternal learns the contours of eternity itself. Form is the instrument, experience the music, and memory the echo that allows the soul to remember—not what it lost, but what it has always been."

The question lingered in the morning air like incense—slow, curling, impossible to rush.

Akanksh looked at Guruji with quiet intensity. "Guruji," he asked, "how does the soul remain untouched while fully participating in the body and mind it animates?"

Guruji closed his eyes for a moment, as if listening to something far older than the question itself. Then he reached down and dipped his fingers into a small bowl of water kept near the altar. Lifting his hand, droplets fell back into the bowl, each one creating a ripple.

"Tell me," he said softly, "did the water lose itself when it formed ripples?"

"No," Akanksh replied.

"And yet," Guruji smiled, "the ripples danced, collided, rose, and disappeared."

He looked around the circle.

"The soul is like the ocean. The body and mind are its waves. Waves rise and fall, crash and dissolve, but the ocean remains vast, unmoved in its depth."

He paused, allowing the words to sink in—not as information, but as remembrance. The morning air seemed to listen with them.

Then Guruji spoke, his voice low and steady, and recited from the **Bhagavad Gita, Chapter 2, Verse 23**:

na enaṁ chhindanti śastrāṇi na enaṁ dahati pāvakaḥ|
na cainaṁ kledayanty āpo na śoṣayati mārutaḥ||

He looked around the circle.

"Krishna is not offering Arjuna poetry to console his sorrow," Guruji said gently. "This is precision—metaphysical accuracy. The soul is not cut by weapons, not burned by fire, not drenched by water, nor dried by wind. It participates fully in life, yet is never altered by what life does."

He let the silence deepen.

"The soul is present in pain, but pain does not belong to it. It witnesses joy, but joy does not define it. What you call suffering happens in the body and the mind. What you *are* stands prior to both."

Guruji leaned forward slightly.

"Consciousness—the symptom of the soul—can be perceived. We can measure awareness, observe thoughts, and study neural signals. But the soul itself cannot be grasped by any instrument, for it is not material. It does not interact with matter the way matter interacts with matter. This is why Krishna says that wind cannot wither it, water cannot moisten it, and fire cannot burn it. The soul belongs to a different order of reality."

After a pause, Guruji continued, quoting **Bhagavad Gita, Chapter 2, Verse 24**:

acchedyo 'yam adāhyo 'yam akledyo 'śoṣya eva ca |
nityaḥ sarva-gataḥ sthāṇur acalo 'yaṁ sanātanaḥ ||

"The soul is unbreakable, incombustible, unwettable, and undryable. It is eternal, all-pervading, immovable, ancient," he said. "Bodies decay, identities fracture, memories fade—but the soul does not age with time. Time moves *inside* the soul, not the other way around."

Guruji then picked up a small clay lamp. Its flame flickered briefly in the passing air, then steadied.

"The **Upanishads** compare the soul to light," he said. "Light enters a room filled with dust, smoke, and shadows—but it does not become dirty. It reveals everything, yet remains untouched. In the same way, the soul illuminates the mind's thoughts, the body's sensations, the ego's stories—without ever becoming them."

Akanksh felt his breath slow, as if something within him had relaxed its long-held grip.

"In the **Puranas**," Guruji continued, "Vishnu reclines upon the cosmic ocean—**Kṣīra Sāgara**—supporting countless universes. Creation arises, dissolves, and arises again, yet Vishnu remains in yogic rest. Awake. Unmoved. That stillness is not withdrawal—it is mastery. That is the soul's true nature."

Then Guruji softly recited **Bhagavad Gita, Chapter 2, Verse 25**:

avyakto 'yam acintyo 'yam avikāryo 'yam ucyate |
tasmād evaṁ viditvainaṁ nānuśocitum arhasi ||

"The soul is invisible, inconceivable, and unchangeable," he explained. "And knowing this, Krishna tells Arjuna—do not grieve. Grief arises only when the imperishable is mistaken for the perishable."

He paused, then added quietly, "The **Kaṭha Upanishad (1.3.10)** explains why the soul escapes the grasp of intellect:

indriyebhyaḥ parā hy arthā arthebhyaś ca paraṁ manaḥ|

manasastu parā buddhir buddher ātmā mahān paraḥ||

'Beyond the senses are their objects. Beyond the objects is the mind. Beyond the mind is the intellect. Beyond even the intellect abides the soul.'"

He smiled, almost tenderly.

"The intellect is brilliant—but it can only reach what belongs to matter. The soul belongs to the eternal. It is not reached by analysis, but by stillness."

Then Guruji added softly, drawing from the **Bible, Ecclesiastes 3:11**:

"He has made everything beautiful in its time. He has also set eternity in the human heart."

"And the Sufi mystic Rumi echoes the same truth," Guruji said, his voice warm:

'You are not a drop in the ocean. You are the entire ocean in a drop.'

He looked at Akanksh and said gently,

"When you stop trying to *touch* the soul, you realise—you have always been *standing as it.*"

Nothing more needed to be said.

Something ancient had been named.

Something eternal had been remembered.

Then Guruji's voice softened, as though stepping onto sacred ground.

"The **Bible** speaks of Christ walking among suffering humanity—hungry, grieving, healing, loving—yet never losing his anchorage in divine awareness. *'I and the Father and I are one,'* Christ declares (**John 10:30**). Though he wept at Lazarus' tomb (**John 11:35**), though he bore anguish and betrayal, his identity was never swallowed by circumstance. He lived fully in the world without being owned by it."

Guruji's gaze rested on Akanksh.

"This is why Christ could say, *'They are in the world, but not of the world'* (**John 17:14–16**). This is not holiness reserved for prophets alone—it is the natural state of the soul when it remembers its source."

He paused, letting the words descend gently.

"And the **Sufis**," Guruji continued, "speak of the reed flute—*ney*—sung of by **Rumi** in the opening of the *Masnavi*:

'Listen to the reed, how it tells a tale, complaining of separations…' (**Masnavi I:1**).

"The flute cries with longing, sorrow, and ecstasy. Its body is hollowed by pain, yet the breath that moves through it remains whole. The song belongs to the flute; the breath belongs to the Eternal."

A long silence followed—thick, alive, reverent.

"The soul does not avoid life to remain pure," Guruji said at last. "It remains pure because purity is its nature. Participation does not stain it—forgetfulness does."

He leaned closer, his eyes softened by compassion.

"When you say, 'I am angry,' the soul is untouched. When you say, 'I am broken,' the soul is untouched. Suffering begins the moment the witness forgets it is witnessing—and mistakes the wave for the ocean."

He smiled gently, almost playfully.

"The soul enters the body the way an actor enters a role—fully, passionately, convincingly—yet never forgets, at the deepest level, that it is not the costume. Krishna hints at this again when he says, *'As a person puts on new garments, giving up old ones, so the soul accepts new bodies'* (**Bhagavad Gita 2:22**)."

Guruji turned toward the ancient banyan tree, its roots descending from the branches like bridges between worlds.

"You are not here to escape the body," he said softly. "You are here to live it so completely that one day—even in the midst of pain, love, and loss—you remember: *I am not what passes. I am what remains.*"

Akanksh bowed his head—not in agreement, but in recognition.

The question had not been answered.

It had been remembered.

Akshatha's question did not arise from curiosity alone; it rose from a quiet ache—the kind that comes after living many moments yet sensing that something deeper is unfolding beneath them.

She asked softly, "Guruji, is experience merely accumulation, or is it a sacred dialogue through which consciousness matures?"

Guruji closed his eyes for a moment, as though listening—not to her, but to time itself.

"Experience," he began, "is not a warehouse where memories are stacked. It is a conversation—alive, intimate, and purposeful—between the soul and existence."

He picked up a smooth river stone, worn round by centuries of water.

"This stone was not polished by collecting water," he said. "It was shaped by *meeting* the river again and again. Each touch was brief, but the dialogue was constant."

He looked at her gently, as if weighing not just her question, but her readiness to receive it.

matra-sparshaas tu kaunteya shitoshna-sukha-duhkha-daah |

agamapayino 'nityas tans-titikshasva bharata | |

Meaning: "O son of Kunti," Krishna says, "the contact of the senses with their objects gives rise to cold and heat, pleasure and pain. They come and go; they are impermanent. Therefore, learn to endure them, O descendant of Bharata."

Guruji let the words settle.

"The human body," he continued, "is a meeting place of five gateways—sight, sound, smell, taste, and touch. Through these doors, the world enters us. When the senses touch their objects, sensations arise: comfort and discomfort, joy and sorrow. But none of these are fixed truths. They are visitors."

He paused, then offered a simple image.

"Cool water delights you in summer and troubles you in winter. The water has not changed—*you* have. Pleasure and pain are not properties of the world; they are reactions within the senses. Like seasons, they arrive, stay briefly, and depart."

His voice grew steadier.

"If the mind clings to pleasure, it fears loss. If it resists pain, it multiplies suffering. Then life becomes a pendulum—swinging endlessly between craving and aversion."

He looked at her again, compassion in his eyes.

"Krishna does not tell Arjuna to escape experience. He asks him to *stand upright within it.* Experience is not meant to enslave consciousness; it is meant to refine it. Endurance here does not mean numbness—it means clarity. Discernment. Depth."

He smiled softly.

"When sensations pass through you without owning you, experience matures into wisdom. And wisdom is not gathered—it is revealed."

Guruji continued, his voice slowing, as though each syllable carried the weight of centuries.

asato mā sad gamaya

tamaso mā jyotir gamaya

mṛtyor mā amrtam gamaya

om sāntih sāntih sāntih

— Brhadaranyaka Upanishad 1.3.28

"Lead us from the unreal to the Real.

Lead us from darkness to Light.

Lead us from death to Immortality.

May there be peace—peace—peace."

He lifted his gaze.

"The Upanishads do not describe life as a problem to be solved," Guruji said, "but as a pilgrimage of recognition. This is not a prayer for new knowledge; it is a yearning to *see rightly*. The unreal is not the world—it is our misreading of it. Darkness is not the absence of light, but the absence of understanding. Death is not the end of the body, but identification with what perishes."

He paused, letting the silence speak.

"Each experience—joy or sorrow, gain or loss—becomes a footstep in this prayer. When resisted, it binds. When listened to, it instructs. Experience, then, is not accumulation; it is *initiation*. It strips illusion, deepens awareness, and slowly turns the seeker toward what does not change."

His voice softened.

"When life is lived as this prayer, even pain becomes a guide—and peace is no longer a destination, but the ground beneath every step."

He gestured toward the sky, now streaked with evening light.

"In the **Puranas**, the avatars of Vishnu descend not because the Divine lacks wisdom, but because wisdom ripens through engagement. Rama learns righteousness through exile; Krishna reveals love through a relationship; Narasimha manifests through devotion tested at the edge of terror. Consciousness matures not in isolation, but in encounter."

Akshatha listened, her eyes moist.

"The **Bible** echoes this truth," Guruji said. "*'Suffering produces perseverance; perseverance, character; and character, hope'* (**Romans 5:3–4**). Experience is not punishment—it is refinement. Even Christ 'grew in wisdom' (**Luke 2:52**), not by avoiding life, but by walking fully within it."

He smiled faintly.

"And the **Sufis**," he added, "say that the soul is wine, and experience is the fermentation. Rumi writes, *'Where there is ruin, there is hope for a treasure'* (*Masnavi*). Without the breaking, the sweetness remains dormant."

Guruji leaned forward.

"When experience is accumulated, it becomes a burden. When it is *received*, it becomes wisdom. The same fire that burns the careless cook perfects the potter's clay."

He placed his hand over his heart.

"Consciousness does not mature by knowing more—but by *meeting itself* through joy, grief, love, failure, and wonder. Each experience asks a question. Awareness is the reply."

A long silence followed.

At last, Guruji spoke, almost in a whisper.

"Experience is not what happens to you. It is what *awakens* through you."

Akshatha lowered her head, not in reverence—but in recognition.

She realised she had not been collecting moments.

She had been in dialogue with eternity.

Apeksha asked, "Guruji, how might our life transform if we understood the mind as a tool or interface, rather than the true self?"

Guruji smiled, as though Apeksha's question had already begun to answer itself within her.

He reached down and gently tapped the wooden desk beside him.

"Child," he said softly, "this table carries books, lamps, and letters—but it never claims authorship of their contents. The mind is much the same. It is a *surface of contact*, not the source of being."

He paused, then spoke slowly, letting the image form.

"When the mind is mistaken for the self, life becomes exhausting. Every thought feels personal. Every emotion becomes identity. Joy inflates the 'I,' pain fractures it, fear commands it. But when the mind is known as an *interface*—a sacred instrument—something profound changes: **you stop living inside reactions and begin standing in awareness**."

He quoted gently from the **Bhagavad Gita (6.5)**, where Krishna speaks of the mind as both friend and enemy:

uddhared atmanatmanam natmanam avasadayet |

atmaiva hyatmano bandhur atmaiva ripur atmanah | |

One must elevate oneself by the mind, not degrade oneself.

The mind can be the friend of the soul—and the mind can be its enemy.

"This," Guruji said, "is not a moral warning—it is a technical instruction. The mind is a tool. When you mistake the tool for the user, the tool controls you."

Guruji spoke with quiet authority, as though weighing each word before offering it.

"On one hand," he said, "the mind is the soul's greatest benefactor. On the other hand, it is its most formidable adversary. No force shapes our destiny more decisively. A disciplined mind becomes a ladder toward clarity and freedom; an undisciplined one becomes a pit where consciousness is slowly dimmed by fear, desire, and restless thought."

He paused, letting the truth settle.

"To befriend the mind, one must first understand its nature. The sages did not speak of the mind as a single, flat entity. They observed it functioning through *four interwoven dimensions*—not separate substances, but different movements of the same inner instrument."

He began to explain, carefully, almost reverently.

"When the mind *generates thoughts*, it is called **manas**—the stream of impressions, doubts, and sensory reactions.

When it *analyses, discriminates, and decides*, it is called **buddhi**—the intellect, the faculty of discernment.

When it *remembers, clings, and forms emotional bonds*, it is called **chitta**—the storehouse of impressions and attachments.

And when it *identifies*—when it says 'I am this body,' 'I am successful,' 'I am wounded,' 'I am superior'—it is called **ahankāra**, the sense of ego."

Guruji lifted his finger gently.

"Do not mistake these as four minds. There are *four functions of one inner apparatus*. Depending on what it is doing, we give it a different name. Together, the scriptures call this entire mechanism the **antahkarana**—the inner instrument."

He smiled faintly.

"This is why different traditions describe it differently. They are not contradicting one another; they are illuminating different angles of the same truth."

He continued:

"The **Pañchadaśī** speaks of the mind as a whole and calls it the cause of bondage when it is turned outward.

The **Yoga Darśana** distinguishes mind, intellect, and ego while analysing how nature binds consciousness.

Shankaracarya, in his precision, describes all four—manas, buddhi, chitta, and ahankāra—to show how the Self becomes entangled when discrimination is lost."

Guruji's tone softened, but his meaning sharpened.

"The word *ego* here must not be confused with modern psychology. Freud used the term to describe a negotiating identity between instinct and social conditioning. The sages meant something deeper: *false identification*. Ahankāra is not pride alone—it is the moment awareness forgets itself and mistakes the instrument for the owner."

He leaned forward slightly.

"When Krishna says, 'Elevate yourself by the mind; do not degrade yourself by the mind' (*Bhagavad Gita 6:5*), he is offering a precise instruction. He is not asking the mind to control itself blindly. He is asking the **higher function of the mind—buddhi, discrimination—to guide the lower function—manas, impulse and reaction**."

He said gently:

"When the intellect governs the mind, the mind becomes a friend.

When the mind overpowers the intellect, it becomes a tyrant.

Freedom does not require destroying the mind.

It requires *placing it in its proper seat.*"

He leaned back, eyes distant, as if remembering an old story.

"In the Upanishads (Katha Upanishad 1.3.3–9)," Guruji said, his voice calm and luminous, "the sages offer one of the most compassionate and precise metaphors ever given to humanity."

Katha Upanishad — Chapter 1, Section 3

Verse 1.3.3

ātmānaṁ rathinaṁ viddhi śarīraṁ ratham eva tu
buddhiṁ tu sārathiṁ viddhi manaḥ pragraham eva ca
Meaning:

Know the Self as the rider, the body as the chariot;

Know the intellect as the charioteer, and the mind as the reins.

Verse 1.3.4

indriyāṇi hayān āhur viṣayāṁs teṣu gocarān

ātmendriya-mano-yuktaṁ bhoktety āhur manīṣiṇaḥ

Meaning:

The senses are said to be the horses, and sense-objects their paths; The Self, united with body, senses, and mind, is called the experiencer by the wise.

Verse 1.3.9

so 'dhvanah pāram āpnoti tad visnoh paramaṁ padam

Meaning:

One who has such understanding reaches the end of the path—

That supreme abode of the All-pervading Reality.

He paused, as if allowing the image to assemble itself within the listener.

"The **body** is the **chariot**—beautiful, powerful, yet inert without guidance.

The **senses** are the **horses**—full of energy, eager, restless, each pulling toward its own desire.

The **mind** is the **reins**—subtle, flexible, capable of directing immense force.

The **intellect** is the **charioteer**—the one who knows the road.

And the **Self** is the **rider**—silent, sovereign, aware."

He smiled gently.

"Now imagine what happens when the reins forget their role and begin to believe, *'I am the rider.'* The horses surge in all directions. One pulls toward pleasure, another toward fear, another toward memory or ambition. The chariot lurches, the path is lost, and exhaustion is mistaken for destiny. This is the state of a life driven by impulse and identity rather than awareness."

Guruji's gaze softened.

"But the reins are not the enemy. The mind was never meant to be silenced or broken. When the reins remember the presence of the rider and respond to the guidance of the charioteer, something extraordinary happens. The same horses that once ran wild now move in harmony. Speed becomes purposeful. Strength becomes grace. The journey becomes meaningful."

He leaned closer, his words almost a whisper.

"The Upanishads are not warning us against the body or the mind. They are reminding us of the **right relationship**. Suffering does not arise because we have a chariot. It arises because we forget who is seated within it."

He said quietly:

"When the mind is treated as an interface, not the Self, life changes.

Thoughts arise, but they no longer rule.

Emotions surge, but they no longer define.

Experiences come and go, but the rider remains unmoved."

A silence followed—dense, alive, reverent.

"The chariot was never meant to run without its rider," Guruji said at last. "And the rider was never meant to abandon the journey."

Apeksha's eyes softened.

"In the **Puranas**," Guruji continued, "Shiva is shown seated in perfect stillness, while his cosmic dance unfolds as Shakti. Movement and silence coexist. The dance does not disturb the stillness. Likewise, thoughts may arise, emotions may surge—but awareness remains untouched when it is not confused with motion."

He turned toward the window, where sunlight filtered through dust motes.

"The **Bible**, too, whispers this truth. 'Be still, and know that I am God' (*Psalm 46:10*). Stillness is not inactivity—it is *dis-identification.* When the mind quiets, something deeper recognises itself."

Then his voice became tender.

"And the **Sufis**, Ah… they say the mind is like a cup dipped into the ocean. The water inside trembles with every wave, but the ocean itself is never disturbed. The seeker suffers only because he thinks he is the cup."

He looked back at Apeksha.

"If the mind is an interface, not the self, then thoughts lose their tyranny. Emotions become messages, not masters. Memory informs, but does not imprison. You still think, feel, plan, and dream—but from *space*, not compulsion."

He smiled gently.

"Anger arises—but you are not angry.

Fear appears—but you are not afraid.

Thoughts pass—but you are not passing."

A long silence followed.

"When this shift occurs," Guruji said finally, "life becomes intimate but not entangling. You participate fully, yet remain inwardly free. The mind becomes a sacred screen through which existence communicates—not a prison in which the soul is confined."

Apeksha lowered her gaze, her breath deep and steady.

Nothing dramatic had changed.

And yet—everything had.

CHAPTER II

Prana, Consciousness, and the Akashic Field

"Thoughts rise like birds in the sky, but the sky does not belong to them. Consciousness remains—vast, untouched, and endlessly open."

– Shree Shambav.

Synopsis

This chapter explores the unseen architecture of existence—where Prana, Consciousness, and the Akashic Field converge to animate life, illuminate experience, and preserve cosmic memory. Through Guruji's calm yet penetrating guidance, the reader is led beyond the visible body into the subtle forces that make living possible. Prana is revealed as the life-current that awakens matter, while consciousness is shown not as thought, but as the luminous field in which all experience arises and dissolves. Beyond both lies the Akashic Field, a vast, formless reservoir where every action, emotion, and intention is eternally recorded—not as memory in the brain, but as vibration in existence itself.

Using poetic storytelling and cross-cultural wisdom, the chapter reframes intuition as remembrance rather than learning, and life as a symphony conducted by invisible currents. It invites the reader to recognise that nothing lived is ever lost—and that awareness itself is the bridge between breath, memory, and meaning.

After the midday meal, after gentle conversations and a brief rest, the seekers returned to the Buddha Hall. The air itself seemed to wait. Cushions were adjusted, breaths softened, and silence slowly ripened into attention. No one spoke. Everyone listened—even before a word was spoken.

After a few minutes, Guruji entered. He bowed slightly to the stillness, then sat. A minute passed. Perhaps longer. In that quiet, something subtle settled, as if the room itself had remembered why it existed.

Then Guruji spoke, his voice calm, measured, and luminous.

"Prana animates the body. Consciousness illumines experience. The Akashic Field remembers all. Together, they form the invisible infrastructure of existence."

He paused.

"This," he said softly, "is the unseen architecture through which life remembers itself."

He lifted his gaze and continued, "The ancient seers declared: *From space arose air… and into space all returns.* What they pointed to was not poetry, but process. Before thought takes form, before emotion finds a name, something already moves."

A hush deepened.

"A subtle current enters the body the way dawn enters a darkened room—not with noise, not with force, but with quiet authority. Breath becomes more than air; it becomes an invitation. In that silent exchange, flesh awakens, the mind brightens, and awareness begins its delicate dance with form."

Guruji leaned forward slightly.

"Life is not assembled—it is conducted. An unseen current animates the body. Consciousness lights the stage upon which experience appears. And beyond both exists a vast, formless memory that holds every gesture existence has ever made. Nothing is lost. Nothing is forgotten. The universe keeps its diary—not in words, but in vibration."

Then he smiled, as if recalling an old friend.

"Let me tell you a story."

"A wandering Sufi once asked a potter, 'What gives the clay its life—the shape or the space within?' The potter said nothing. He lifted an empty vessel and placed it before the Sufi. 'Strike it,' he said."

Guruji gently tapped the floor with his staff, mimicking the sound.

"The vessel rang—clear, hollow, alive. And the potter whispered, 'This is where the song lives.'"

He let the image breathe.

"So it is with life. Prana flows like an unseen river through the body, animating it from within. Consciousness is the open sky in which every sensation, thought, and emotion arises and dissolves. And beyond both—like an eternal echo chamber—exists a vast field that remembers every breath ever taken, every prayer ever whispered, every tear that ever touched the earth."

His voice softened.

"When a truth feels strangely familiar, when wisdom rises without effort, it is not imagination. It is recognition. The soul is not learning—it is remembering."

Guruji looked around the hall, meeting each pair of eyes not as teacher to student, but as one remembering to another.

Then, gently, he placed four questions into the silence—like seeds into fertile soil:

"How does life-force enter matter?"

"Where does memory exist beyond the brain?"

"Why do some truths feel remembered, not learned?"

"And is intuition the soul reading its own record?"

The hall remained silent.

But within that silence, something ancient stirred.

Roopa asked, "Guruji, if life-force animates all matter, what truly distinguishes a living body from an inert form, beyond mere chemistry?"

Roopa's question lingered in the hall like incense after a flame has been extinguished—soft, searching, impossible to ignore.

Guruji closed his eyes, as though listening to something older than sound. When he spoke, his voice carried the stillness of deep waters.

"Chemistry can assemble the clay," he said gently, "but it cannot invite the dancer."

He gestured toward the window, where a leaf trembled in the afternoon breeze.

"The elements that form a living body are the same elements that lie in dust, stone, and ash. Carbon, calcium, water, minerals—nothing new is added. And yet," he paused, "one breath transforms matter into life. When that breath departs, the body remains chemically complete, but something essential is missing."

He leaned forward.

"That missing presence is **Prana**—the life-current that enters matter not as force, but as permission."

The Lamp and the Flame

Guruji lifted an unlit oil lamp from beside him.

"This lamp," he said, "has oil, a wick, and perfect structure. Chemistry would say it is ready. But until fire touches it, there is no light."

He lit the wick. The flame rose silently.

"The flame does not *belong* to the lamp, yet without the lamp it cannot appear. When the flame departs, the lamp is not broken—only empty."

He looked at Roopa.

"The body is the lamp. Prana is the flame. Consciousness is the light it gives."

Guruji said, "Life is not held together by organs, but by breath. When Prana departs, the eyes remain, yet cannot see; the ears remain, yet cannot hear. Life withdraws as quietly as it entered."

He smiled softly.

"Prana does not announce itself. It simply arrives—and suddenly, the universe begins to speak through the body."

Krishna's Whisper in the Gita

Guruji's voice softened, as though he were no longer teaching but remembering aloud.

"In the Bhagavad Gita," he said, "Krishna does not speak of the soul in metaphor alone—he speaks with surgical clarity. He draws a line between what acts and what *is*."

Guruji recited quietly:

Bhagavad Gita, Chapter 2, Verse 19

ya enam vetti hantāraṁ yaśh chainaṁ manyate hatam |

ubhau tau na vijānīto nāyaṁ hanti na hanyate ||

"Those who believe the soul kills, and those who believe it can be killed—both misunderstand. The soul neither slays nor is slain."

Guruji looked around the hall.

"The body moves. The hands act. The voice speaks. Yet the animating presence remains untouched. Action belongs to nature; witnessing belongs to the soul."

He continued:

Bhagavad Gita, Chapter 2, Verse 20

na jāyate mriyate vā kadāchin

nāyaṁ bhūtvā bhavitā vā na bhūyaḥ

ajo nityaḥ śhāśhvato 'yaṁ purāṇo

na hanyate hanyamāne śharīre

"The soul is never born, nor does it ever die. It does not come into being, nor does it cease to be. Unborn, eternal, immortal, and ancient, it is not destroyed when the body is destroyed."

Guruji paused, letting the words settle.

"What we call birth and death," he said, "are movements of the body alone. The soul does not undergo the six transformations—existence in the womb, birth, growth, reproduction, decline, and death. These belong to matter, not to consciousness."

He smiled gently.

"Death is not the end of the self. It is merely the changing of instruments."

The Echo in the Upanishads

"The Upanishads echo this truth with the same unwavering certainty," Guruji continued.

He recited:

Kaṭha Upanishad, 1.2.18

na jāyate mriyate vā vipaśhchin

nāyaṁ kutaśhchin na babhūva kaśhchit

ajo nityaḥ śhāśhvato 'yaṁ purāṇo

na hanyate hanyamāne śharīre

"The soul is not born, nor does it die. It did not arise from anything, nor did anything arise from it. Unborn, eternal, everlasting, and ancient, it is not slain when the body is slain."

Guruji's eyes were luminous.

"This is not philosophy," he said. "This is remembrance."

He added softly:

Brihadāranyaka Upanishad, 4.4.25

sa vā esha mahān aja ātmā

ajaro 'maro 'mrito 'bhayah

"The Self is great—unborn, undecaying, immortal, fearless."

The Living Insight

"Prana," Guruji said, "is the bridge that allows the immortal to touch the mortal. It animates the body without binding the soul. The soul participates in life without being altered by it—like the sky holding storms without ever becoming wet."

He leaned slightly forward.

"When this is known—not merely believed—fear loosens its grip. Grief softens. And life is lived more fully, because one no longer mistakes the passing costume for the eternal wearer."

He paused.

"Chemistry explains *how* the body functions. Prana explains *why* it awakens."

The Biblical Breath

"The Bible tells us that the first human was formed from dust," Guruji said, his voice reverent, "but dust alone did not live. Life began when breath was breathed into it. Not instruction. Not command. Breath."

He looked around the hall.

"Across traditions, breath is not air—it is spirit in motion."

The Sufi's Reed

"And the Sufis," he added with a smile, "speak of the reed flute. Hollow, lifeless, ordinary—until breath enters. Then it weeps, sings, remembers God."

He closed his eyes briefly.

"The reed does not create the song. It allows it."

The Living Difference

Guruji's voice softened.

"What distinguishes a living body from an inert form is not complexity—it is **listening**. A living body is one that is being played by existence."

He met Roopa's gaze.

"When Prana flows, the body is not merely matter—it becomes a conversation between the visible and the invisible."

A silence followed, full and luminous.

"Life," Guruji said, "is not chemistry perfected. It is consciousness invited."

Roopa bowed her head—not because she understood fully, but because something within her had begun to breathe more deeply.

The question had found its answer—not in words, but in aliveness.

Akshaya asked softly, "Guruji, if consciousness is a boundless field, not a fleeting thought, where does awareness dwell—inside us, or in something larger than the mind?"

Guruji closed his eyes, as though listening—not to the question, but to the silence behind it.

When he opened them, his gaze rested gently on Akshaya.

"Tell me," he asked softly, "where does the sky reside? Inside the clouds—or beyond them?"

Akshaya remained quiet.

"The mind," Guruji continued, "is like a clouded sky. Thoughts drift, emotions gather, memories rain and pass. But awareness—the one that *knows* the clouds—is never contained by them."

He leaned forward slightly, his voice warm, steady.

"In the **Bhagavad Gita (6.29),** Krishna describes the vision of the true yogi—one whose consciousness has been unified through yoga. Such a one *sees the Self abiding in all beings, and all beings abiding in the Self.* This is not poetic exaggeration or mystical metaphor. It is a **radical ontological claim**: awareness does not reside inside the mind; rather, the mind arises *within* awareness.

sarva-bhuta-stham atmanam sarva-bhutani chatmani |

ikshate yoga-yuktatma sarvatra sama-darshanah | |

“One who is established in yoga perceives the Self present in all beings, and all beings present in the Self. Such a person sees with equal vision everywhere.”

Guruji said, “Just as the sun remains unmoving in the sky yet illuminates everything by its rays, so the Supreme Consciousness, while untouched and indivisible, pervades and sustains all existence through its many energies. The yogi does not *imagine* this unity—he *sees* it. In the light of realised knowledge, every form is recognised as a movement within the One, and every being as a living expression of the Divine.”

He picked up a brass bowl filled with water and held it up so the light reflected on its surface.

“Look,” he said. “The moon appears in this water. If the water trembles, the reflection shakes. But does the moon tremble in the sky?”

Akshaya shook his head.

“So it is with awareness,” Guruji said. “Thought agitates the mind, emotion disturbs the surface—but awareness itself remains untouched. The mind is a lens, not the source.”

The Upanishads Vision

"In the **Brihadaranyaka Upanishad (3.8.8),"** Guruji continued,
"the sages speak of *That* which sees, yet cannot be seen; hears, yet cannot be heard; thinks, yet cannot be thought."

He then recited the ancient words addressed to Gārgī:

sa hovāca, etadvai tadakśaraḥ, gārgi brāhmaṇā abhivadanti, asthūlamanaṇvahrasvamadīrghamalohitamasnehamacchāyama tamo'-
vāyvanākāśamasaṅgamacakśuṣkamaśrotramavāgamano'-tejaskamaprāṇamamukhamamātramanantaramabāhyam, na tadaśnāti kiṃcana, na tadaśnāti kaśсana | |

"O Gargi," the knowers of Brahman declare, "this is the **Immutable Reality**.

It is neither gross nor subtle, neither short nor long.

It has no colour, no texture, no shadow, no darkness.

It is not air, nor space—yet nothing is outside it.

It is unattached, without taste or smell, without eyes or ears,

without speech or mind, without light or vital breath.

It has no measure, no inside or outside.

It does not consume anything, nor can anything consume it."

Guruji paused, then said softly,

"This is not a negation born of ignorance—it is a negation born of reverence. The sages remove every attribute, not because the Truth is empty, but because it is **too vast to be confined by form**."

He looked at the listeners with gentle clarity.

"What sees cannot itself be seen. What knows cannot itself be an object of knowledge. The Upanishads do not ask us to *understand* this Reality—but to **stand as it**."

He smiled gently.

"Awareness cannot be located because it is not an object. Location belongs to things that can be pointed to. Awareness is what allows pointing to happen."

He paused, then added,

"The **Mandukya Upanishad** declares that consciousness is not waking, not dreaming, not deep sleep—but *that* in which all three appear. Where would you place such a thing? Inside the mind? Or as the ground in which the mind itself arises?"

Echoes

Guruji's voice softened further.

"In the **Bible**, when Moses asks God for His name, the answer is not a description, not a location, not a form—only *'I AM'* (Exodus 3:14). Not *I think*, not *I act*, not *I appear*—but *I AM.* Pure awareness, self-existing."

He turned slightly, as if listening to another current.

"And the Sufis," he said, smiling, "tell us: *'You are not a drop in the ocean. You are the ocean in a drop.'* Awareness does not sit inside the heart or the head—it expresses itself *as* the heart, *as* the head, *as* every form it illumines."

The Living Answer

Guruji looked directly at Akshaya.

"When you ask, 'Where does awareness reside?' notice this—*what is aware of the question itself?* Is it inside the thought, or does the thought rise within it?"

He let the silence answer first.

"Awareness resides nowhere—because it is everywhere. It is not confined to the mind, yet it knows the mind intimately. It is not bound to the body, yet it animates every cell."

He spoke more softly now.

"When you sit quietly and notice your breath, your thoughts, your emotions—there is something that watches without effort. That watcher does not move when the mind moves. That is not *in* you. That is what you are."

Guruji smiled.

"The moment you stop searching for awareness as an object, you awaken as the field itself."

Akshaya lowered his eyes—not in confusion, but in stillness.

The question had dissolved.

What remained was presence—vast, silent, unmistakably home.

Padma's question lingered in the hall like incense after the flame had vanished.

"Guruji," she asked softly, "how does memory persist when the body changes, the brain forgets, and yet insight reappears across lifetimes and cultures?"

Guruji closed his eyes for a moment.

The River That Forgets Its Banks

Guruji began, "What you call memory is not a single thing. There is **memory of the flesh**, **memory of the mind**, and **memory of being**."

He picked up a small brass bowl and poured water into it.

"This water remembers nothing of the river it came from. Once it is poured, its shape changes. But does the river forget itself because the water has changed containers?"

The body is like the bowl. The brain is like the ripples on the surface. When the bowl breaks, the water returns to the river. The *container* forgets—but the **source remembers**.

What the Gita Calls the Unbroken Thread

Guruji's voice softened, as if he were careful not to disturb something delicate and ancient.

"In the **Bhagavad Gita (15.8)**," he said, "Krishna offers one of the most intimate images of continuity ever given to humanity. He does not speak of memory as a ledger or a record, but as a **fragrance**."

śarīram yad avāpnoti yac cāpy utkramatīśvaraḥ

gṛhītvaitāni saṁyāti vāyur gandhān ivāśayāt

"Just as the wind carries fragrance from one place to another," Guruji explained, "so does the embodied soul carry the mind and senses when it leaves one body and enters another."

He paused, letting the image breathe.

"Notice," he added, "the wind does not carry the flower—only its **essence**. In the same way, the soul does not transport memories as photographs. It carries **impressions**—subtle tendencies, emotional residues, unfinished longings, half-sung melodies of being."

The Child Who Dreamed of Colours

Guruji then told a story.

In a quiet village, a child was born blind. From birth, he had never seen the sun, the sky, or the faces of those who loved him. Yet each night, he would awaken startled, speaking of colours.

"Mother," he once said, "why was the sky purple in my dream?"

His mother smiled through tears. "The sky has no colour for you, my son."

"But it did in my dream," the boy insisted. "I was flying, and below me were fields—golden, green, endless."

The village doctor dismissed it as imagination. The priest called it symbolism. But an old wandering monk who happened to pass through listened quietly.

"Do you know," the monk said, "why a bird born in a cage still dreams of the sky?"

The mother shook her head.

"Because the sky is not learned," he replied. "It is **remembered**."

Guruji looked around the hall.

"Dreams," he said, "are not limited by this lifetime's senses. They arise from the **subtle mind**, which the soul carries across bodies. That is why even one born blind may dream of vision—not because the eyes remember, but because **consciousness does**."

The State That Becomes the Destination

Guruji then quoted another verse, his tone now solemn.

"In **Bhagavad Gita (8.6)**, Krishna reveals a law as precise as gravity and as merciful as grace."

yam yam vā'pi smaran bhāvam tyajaty ante kalevaram |

tam tam evaiti kaunteya sadā tad-bhāva-bhāvitah | |

"Whatever state of being one remembers at the time of leaving the body," "that state one enters next."

"This," Guruji clarified, "is not about a single thought at the final moment. Death does not listen to last-minute prayers alone. It listens to the **habitual music of the mind**."

He smiled gently.

"If you hear a flute playing from a house every day for years, you will not be surprised to hear it on the final evening. Likewise, the mind at death does not improvise—it **reveals what it has rehearsed**."

Not Images, but Patterns

"These are not memories stored like pictures in the brain," Guruji continued.

"They are **tendencies**—what the Gita calls *bhāva*. The brain records facts. The soul carries **patterns**."

Fear carried long enough becomes instinct. Love practised deeply becomes refuge. Anger fed repeatedly becomes direction. Devotion lived sincerely becomes home.

"The next birth," Guruji said, "is not a reward or punishment. It is a **continuation**."

The Traveller and the Packed Luggage

He concluded with another image.

"When we plan a journey," Guruji said, "we do not decide our destination after boarding the train. We pack our luggage beforehand."

"In the same way," he added softly, "one cannot live in distraction and expect clarity at death, nor live in fear and expect freedom beyond it."

Life, he reminded them, is preparation—not for death, but for **continuity**.

"The soul travels light," Guruji said at last. "But whatever fragrance you have cultivated—that alone goes with you."

The Upanishadic Seed Memory

He turned to Padma and smiled, as though inviting her into a quiet secret.

"The **Chāndogya Upanishad** speaks of a banyan seed," he said, holding his fingers close together, "so small it appears almost empty. If you split it open, you find nothing inside—no roots, no trunk, no leaves."

He paused, then asked gently, "And yet, from this seeming nothingness rises a vast tree—thousands of branches, countless leaves, shelter for generations. So tell me, Padma… where was the tree hiding?"

He answered before she could speak.

"Not in form," he said softly, "but in **potential**."

"Memory works the same way," Guruji continued. "Wisdom does not survive as stored information, travelling intact from one body to another. It survives as **seed-knowledge**—compressed, silent, waiting."

"When the conditions are right—when sincerity, suffering, love, or stillness prepare the soil—that seed opens. And what unfolds feels strangely familiar, as though one is not discovering truth for the first time, but **recognising** it."

This is why wisdom reappears across lifetimes and cultures.

Sages in India, prophets in the desert, mystics in monasteries, and Sufis in bustling marketplaces speak the same truths in different tongues. They are not copying one another. They are not inheriting ideas.

"They are drawing water," Guruji said, "from the same unseen well."

Truth does not travel from person to person. It **flowers wherever consciousness becomes ready to remember its own depth**.

The Bible's Book of Remembrance

"In the Book of *Jeremiah*," Guruji said softly, "the Divine declares, *'Before I formed you in the womb, I knew you'* (Jeremiah 1:5). And in *Ecclesiastes* we read, *'There is nothing new under the sun'* (Ecclesiastes 1:9)."

He let the words settle, then asked gently, "What do these verses reveal?"

"They tell us that creation does not improvise—it **remembers**. Life is not a random sequence of accidents, nor a frantic act of invention. It is an unfolding of what already exists in the deeper order of being."

"What appears new is only a new **appearance** of an ancient truth. Forms change, faces change, languages change—but the wisdom moving through them remains the same."

"The prophets," Guruji continued, "did not *learn* truth the way students memorise lessons. They **recognised** it—just as the heart recognises love without being taught how."

"They were not gathering ideas. They were awakening to a knowing that had always known them."

"In this sense," he said, "memory is not held in the brain alone. It is held in **being itself**—and revelation is simply the moment when the soul remembers what it never truly forgot."

The Sufi Story of the Forgotten Name

Guruji smiled and shared a Sufi tale.

A master once asked his disciple, "Why do you seek God?"

The disciple bowed and said, "Because I have forgotten Him."

The master laughed softly. "If you had truly forgotten, you would not be searching. One does not yearn for what has never been known. Your longing itself is the memory."

He fell silent, allowing the insight to ripen.

"True remembrance," Guruji continued, "does not belong to the brain. It belongs to **Being**. The brain stores information; Being carries recognition."

"This is why insight can rise suddenly, without effort or instruction. Why does truth sometimes feel familiar the moment it is heard. Why longing appears before understanding."

"Intuition, devotion, and sudden clarity are not accidents," he said gently. "They are echoes—ripples from a depth that has always known."

"When consciousness turns inward, it is not discovering something new. It is hearing its own forgotten name being spoken again."

The hall remained silent—not empty, but listening.

Why Wisdom Feels Familiar

"Have you noticed," Guruji asked Padma, "that when a great truth is spoken, it does not surprise you? It **recognises you**."

This is because awareness carries what the **Brhadaranyaka Upanishad** calls *smṛti beyond time*—a knowing untouched by birth or death. The mind may forget names and faces, but consciousness does not forget **its own nature**.

The Invisible Archive

"So where does memory truly live?" Guruji said.

"Not in neurons alone. Not in books alone. It lives in what the sages called **Akasha**, what mystics called the **Book of Life**, what Sufis called the **Hidden Tablet**, and what modern seekers glimpse as a **field of consciousness**."

"When insight reappears across lifetimes and cultures, it is not a reincarnation of persons—it is **a recurrence of truth**. The lamp may change, but the flame recognises itself."

Guruji looked at Padma with quiet affection.

"You are not discovering wisdom for the first time," he said softly.

"You are remembering what you have always been."

Vasudeva asked, "Guruji, when intuition speaks beyond logic, is the soul drawing from a deeper archive of knowing rather than creating a new conclusion?"

Guruji closed his eyes for a moment, as if listening inwardly before speaking.

"Yes, Vasudeva," he said softly. "When intuition speaks without logic, it is not guessing—it is **remembering**."

He reached for a lamp beside him and lit it. The flame rose silently.

"Does the flame debate before giving light?" Guruji asked. "Does it calculate whether darkness deserves illumination? No, light knows its work without reasoning. Intuition is like this flame—knowledge that does not argue, because it does not arrive through steps."

The Gita's Silent Knowing

"In the Bhagavad Gita Chapter 2 Verse 24," Guruji continued, his voice steady and precise,

achchhedyo 'yam adahyo 'yam akledyo 'shoshya eva cha |

nityah sarva-gatah sthanur achalo 'yam sanatanah | |

Meaning: The soul is unbreakable and incombustible; it can neither be dampened nor dried. It is eternal, all-pervading, unchanging, immovable, and primordial.

"Here," Guruji explained, "Krishna names the soul *avikārya*—unchangeable—and *sarva-gata*—present everywhere. What is everywhere does not need to travel to know. What is unchanging does not need to arrive at conclusions."

He paused, letting the words settle.

"Logic belongs to the mind," he said, "and the mind moves—step by step, question by question, from one point to another. Intuition belongs to the soul, which already abides at the centre."

"When intuition arises," Guruji continued softly, "the soul is not forming a new opinion. It is **recognising** what has always been known. It is accessing a deeper archive of knowing—one that exists beyond time, beyond memory, beyond thought."

"Reason discovers," he concluded.

"But intuition remembers."

The Upanishadic Archive of Knowing

"The Upanishads call this archive *Smṛti*," Guruji said gently, "not memory as mere recollection, but remembrance as recognition—knowing again what was never truly lost."

"In the *Kena Upanishad*," he continued, *'That which cannot be thought by the mind, but by which the mind is able to think—know That to be Brahman.' (Kena Upanishad 1.6)*

Kena Upanishad 1.6

yan manasā na manute yenāhur mano matam |

tad eva brahma tvaṁ viddhi nedaṁ yad idam upāsate | |

Meaning: That which the mind cannot comprehend, but by which the mind is enabled to think—know That alone as Brahman, and not this which people worship as an object.

"This single line," Guruji explained, "draws a sacred boundary. The mind is an instrument of thinking, but it is not the source of knowing. What empowers the mind to think must exist prior to thought itself."

He paused, then added with quiet clarity, "Intuition does not arise **from** the mind. It passes **through** the mind—like a wind moving through an open window. The window does not create the breeze; it only allows its passage."

Turning to Vasudeva, his gaze steady and kind, Guruji said, "When insight arrives complete—without effort, without argument, without proof—it is not imagination. It is the soul reopening an ancient manuscript, written long before this lifetime began."

"You are not inventing truth," he said.

"You are remembering it."

A Story from the Puranas

"In the Puranas," Guruji said, "there is a story of Narada, the divine sage. He travels across worlds carrying wisdom, yet he never claims authorship. When asked how he knows what he knows, Narada replies, 'I listen.'"

"Listen to what?" Vasudeva asked softly.

"To the vibration of truth itself," Guruji answered. "Narada does not invent wisdom. He tunes into it."

"So it is with intuition. The soul does not *manufacture* truth—it **resonates** with it."

The Bible's Still Small Voice

Guruji said, "In the Bible, the prophet Elijah waits for God in wind, fire, and earthquake—but God does not appear. Finally, there comes a *still, small voice* (1 Kings 19:12)."

"That voice did not argue. It did not explain. It simply **was**."

"Intuition speaks in this way—not loudly, not persuasively, but with a quiet authority that asks for trust, not proof."

The Sufi Mirror

Guruji smiled and shared a Sufi parable.

A seeker once asked a Sufi master, "How do I know when intuition is true?"

The master handed him a mirror and said, "When you look into it, do you debate whether the reflection is yours?"

"No," the seeker replied.

"Why?"

"Because I recognise myself."

The master nodded. "That recognition is intuition."

Guruji leaned forward.

"The brain stores information like a library. The soul carries knowing like the **earth carries seeds**. When the season is right, the seed breaks open—not because it learned how, but because it remembered what it is."

"This is why intuition often arrives whole, immediate, and undeniable. It is not a conclusion reached—it is a **truth resurfacing**."

He said gently:

"Logic builds bridges step by step. Intuition reminds you that you were already standing on the other shore."

Vasudeva bowed—not in certainty, but in quiet trust.

CHAPTER III

The Mathematics of Karma

"Liberation is not the erasure of karma—it is the wisdom that no longer creates more."

– Shree Shambav.

Synopsis

The chapter delves into how gratitude becomes most meaningful not in comfort, but in chaos. When life strips away the predictable and the pleasant, gratitude emerges as a quiet inner rebellion—a choice to perceive purpose amid pain. Adversity often blinds us to beauty, yet those who pause to thank even the breaking find themselves transformed by it.

Through spiritual wisdom and psychological insight, this chapter explores how gratitude reframes suffering: from punishment to purification, from endings to evolutions. It teaches that being thankful during storms isn't denial—it's alignment. The storm, after all, doesn't come to destroy; it comes to cleanse.

Readers are guided through emotional reframing, subtle self-dialogue, and the alchemy of acceptance. Through personal reflection and practical steps, they discover that pain and grace coexist in the same space—and that the heart, when grateful, becomes unbreakable.

Ultimately, this chapter isn't about escaping pain but seeing through it—until light shines from within the storm itself.

After the evening coffee break, the devotees reassembled in Buddha Hall, their footsteps softer now, as though the floor itself were sacred. The day had peeled layers from their certainties; conversations had slowed, eyes had deepened. They waited—not impatiently, but inwardly—for Guruji.

He arrived without announcement and took his seat in silence. His gaze rested on the far edge of the horizon, where the last gold of evening was dissolving into indigo. Dusk hovered like a held breath. No one spoke. Even restlessness seemed to bow.

Then Guruji began—his voice low, steady, carrying both compassion and inevitability.

"At dawn," he said, "when shadows are longest, and light is still learning how to arrive, a temple bell rings. Its sound moves outward—touching stone, air, water, skin. Then it fades. Yet it does not disappear. The vibration settles into the unseen."

He paused, letting the image travel through the hall.

"So it is with action. Every thought you think, every word you speak, every choice you make sends a pulse into existence. Some echoes return swiftly. Others take longer routes—through years, through bodies, sometimes through lifetimes—waiting for the right moment, the right circumstance, the right heart."

Karma, Guruji explained, is this quiet continuity. Not a ledger of reward and punishment, but memory in motion.

"Karma is not cruelty," he said softly. "It is coherence. The universe remembers what we try to forget."

In the Bhagavad Gita, Krishna speaks of action that binds and action that liberates—not because of what is done, but because of how and from where it is done. Action without awareness tightens the knot. Action offered with clarity loosens it. Karma is not a moral judgment; it is an energetic consequence.

"In the Puranas," Guruji continued, "kings rise and fall not because fate is harsh, but because tendencies mature. A seed does not sprout the day it is planted. It waits. So do impressions."

He leaned forward slightly.

"Karma is not reward or punishment—it is continuity. The soul carries unfinished learning forward, like equations seeking balance. It is the universe seeking completion."

Then he raised his hand gently. "To understand this, we must see karma in four forms."

Sanchita—the vast storehouse. All accumulated impressions from countless lives, resting like unread books in a cosmic library.

Prarabdha—the portion selected for this life. Not all at once. Just enough weight to grow strength. Just enough resistance to awaken intelligence.

Kriyamana—what you are doing now. Every response, every intention, every act of awareness or avoidance.

Agami—the future being written silently, even as you listen.

"These are not four karmas," Guruji said. "They are four movements of one river."

Then he smiled faintly. "Let me tell you a story."

"An old accountant once kept records for an entire kingdom. His books were vast—numbers upon numbers, transactions spanning decades. When someone asked him how he remembered so much, he replied, 'I do not remember them. They remember me.'"

The hall was very still.

"The soul," Guruji said, "is such an accountant. Nothing it encounters is accidental. What appears as fortune or misfortune is often an unfinished sentence seeking its final word. Accumulated tendencies lie like unread pages. From these, a few chapters are chosen for this life—just enough sorrow to soften pride, just enough joy to keep faith alive."

"In living them," he continued, "new lines are written—lines that shape futures not yet imagined."

The Bible echoes this in its own language: *What a person sows, that shall they also reap.* Not as a threat—but as a description. The field responds to the seed.

Sufi mystics say the same in poetry: *What you throw into the well of the world echoes back as your destiny.*

"Karma is not fate carved in stone," Guruji said. "It is a living equation—constantly recalculated by awareness. Destiny sets the conditions. Consciousness chooses the response."

He paused, eyes moving across the hall, resting briefly on each face as though recognising something ancient in them.

"This is why suffering may repeat across lifetimes—not because the soul is punished, but because the lesson was not yet completed. This is why free will exists within destiny—not to erase the past, but to redeem it."

He let the silence return, then asked quietly—questions that did not demand answers, but recognition:

"Why does suffering repeat across lifetimes?

Can free will exist within destiny?

Who selects Prarabdha karma—the universe, or the soul itself?

And if all is chosen, what, then, is liberation?"

Somewhere outside, a bell rang—once—and faded.

Kiran asked, "Guruji, if karma is continuity rather than judgment, how does perceiving its true structure change the way we relate to both suffering and joy?"

Guruji closed his eyes, as if listening to something older than the question. When he spoke, his voice was low and steady, like a river that knows its path.

"Kiran," he said, "when a child touches fire and is burned, does the fire punish the child—or does it teach? The fire does not remember the child. The fire only reveals its nature. Karma is like that. It does not sit in judgment; it reflects understanding."

He lifted a small brass bowl filled with water and dropped a stone into it. Ripples spread outward, touched the edges, then returned inward.

Guruji said, "In the Bhagavad Gita, Krishna tells Arjuna that action binds only when one claims ownership of it, and action liberates when it is offered without attachment."

Guruji, after a pause, said, "Suffering is not sent to hurt you; it arrives to complete a movement already set in motion. Joy, too, is not a reward—it is a resonance with harmony."

He smiled softly.

"The Puranas speak of karma as a wheel, not a whip. A wheel turns so that movement may continue. If the wheel stopped, life would stagnate. What you call pain is often friction—the resistance that tells you where growth is required."

Guruji then told a story.

A potter once complained to his teacher, "Every time I shape a pot, the wheel shakes and my hands ache."

The teacher replied, "If the wheel did not turn and the clay did not resist, you would have nothing but a lump of mud. It is the turning that gives form, and the resistance that gives strength."

"So it is with karma," Guruji said. "Suffering shapes the soul; joy confirms its alignment. Both are teachers."

He paused, then continued.

"The Upanishads remind us that the Self is untouched, even as experiences rise and fall. Pain belongs to the field of learning, not to the essence of who you are. When this is known, suffering loses its cruelty. It becomes instruction."

"And the Bible," Guruji added, "speaks of seeds and harvests—not as punishment, but as an unbroken law of life. What is sown must grow. Yet the farmer does not resent the soil for demanding patience, labour, and time. He understands seasons, not judgment."

He continued gently, "In the Letter to the Galatians, it is said: *Do not be deceived—what a person sows, that he will also reap*. And again, *let us not grow weary in doing good, for in due season we shall reap if we do not lose heart* (Galatians 6:7, 9). The emphasis is not fear, but perseverance."

"Paul echoes the same wisdom when he writes that one who sows reaps sparingly reaps sparingly, and one who sows generously reaps generously. The Source that provides seed also enlarges the harvest of righteousness (2 Corinthians 9:6, 10). Karma here is not divine bookkeeping—it is the quiet assurance that effort ripens."

Guruji smiled.

"And Christ himself spoke of seeds falling on different kinds of soil. Some seeds perish, others multiply thirty, sixty, even a hundredfold—not because the seed was judged, but because the ground was ready (Matthew 13:8)."

He said softly, "Life does not punish. It cultivates. What you suffer teaches you how to prepare the soil. What you rejoice in shows you what is already aligned."

From the Sufis, Guruji borrowed another image.

"They say life is a polishing stone. Each hardship smooths a rough edge. The stone does not love or hate the jewel—it only reveals its brilliance."

He looked directly at Kiran.

"When you understand the structure of karma, joy humbles you and suffering matures you. You stop asking, 'Why is this happening to me?' and begin asking, 'What is being completed through me?'"

His voice softened.

"Then suffering no longer feels like betrayal, and joy no longer feels like possession. Both become movements of wisdom."

Guruji fell silent.

Kiran did not feel consoled.

He felt strengthened.

Vidyarthi asked softly, "Guruji, when certain patterns echo through generations, are they burdens, or gentle calls to complete lessons our souls once left open?"

Guruji's gaze rested on Vidyarthi—not as a teacher correcting a question, but as a witness recognising a truth already stirring within the asker.

"Patterns do not repeat to punish," he said softly. "They return to be understood."

He picked up a piece of chalk and drew a circle on the floor.

"In the **Bhagavad Gita**, Krishna never speaks of karma as vengeance. He speaks of **bandha**—bondage born of ignorance—and **moksha**—release born of understanding. Karma is not a whip; it is a mirror."

He turned to Vidyarthi and said gently,

'Action binds only when it is performed without understanding.

When the same action is seen clearly, it liberates.'

This spirit is found throughout the Gita. In **Chapter 4, Shloka 18**, Krishna says:

Karmany akarma yah pasyed akarmani ca karma yah|
Sa buddhimān manushyeshu sa yuktah kritsna-karma-krit'||

"One who sees inaction in action, and action in inaction, is wise among humans; such a one is liberated though engaged in all actions."

Guruji explained, "Suffering repeats not because the soul is guilty, but because the lesson has not yet been *seen.* Consciousness knocks again at a door it once passed without entering."

He paused, allowing the words to settle.

"In **Chapter 5, Shloka 17**, Krishna tells us that liberation comes when understanding dawns:

Tad-buddhayas tad-ātmānas tan-nisthās tat-parāyanāh
Gacchanty apunar-āvrttim jnāna-nirdhūta-kalmasāh

'Those whose intellect is absorbed in That, whose self is rooted in That, who are devoted to That—freed from ignorance by knowledge—do not return again.'

"When ignorance dissolves," Guruji said softly, "repetition dissolves with it."

He then turned inward, as if walking ancient corridors of silence.

"The **Upanishads** speak even more directly. They do not say the soul returns because it is broken, but because it has not yet recognised its wholeness."

Guruji quoted from the **Chandogya Upanishad (6.8.7)**:

'Tat tvam asi' — *'That Thou Art.'*

"And from the **Brihadaranyaka Upanishad (4.4.5)**," he continued:

'As is one's desire, so is one's will;
As is the will, so is the deed;
As is the deed, so is the destiny.'

"The soul," Guruji explained, "returns like a student repeating a lesson—not because the teacher is angry, but because understanding has not yet flowered. The curriculum does not change until comprehension dawns."

He smiled faintly, and his voice took on the texture of a story remembered across centuries.

"In the **Puranas**, there is the story of **King Bharata**, told in the **Srimad Bhagavatam, Canto 5, Chapters 7–8**. Bharata ruled wisely, renounced his kingdom, and lived as an ascetic. Yet in his final days, his heart became tenderly attached to a helpless deer."

Guruji's eyes softened.

"That attachment was not punished. It was *completed.* Bharata was reborn as a deer—fully conscious of his past—so that the unfinished seeing could be finished.

Later, he returned as **Jada Bharata**, utterly detached, awake, free."

He leaned forward slightly.

"What repeats is not sin. What repeats is *unfinished seeing*. Karma is compassion that refuses to abandon the lesson halfway."

Then Guruji turned toward the light streaming through the window.

"Even the **Bible** understands this truth, though it speaks in a different tongue."

He continued,

"Look at **Joseph**, whose story unfolds in **Genesis Chapters 37–50**. Betrayed by his brothers, sold into slavery, falsely accused, imprisoned, forgotten—each descent looked like the same suffering returning again and again."

Guruji's voice deepened.

"But each repetition refined him. Betrayal taught him discernment. Prison taught him humility. Forgetting taught him patience. By the time he stood before Pharaoh, Joseph could interpret dreams—not only because of a divine gift, but because suffering had carved space within him."

Guruji quoted **Genesis 50:20**:

'You intended to harm me, but God intended it for good, to accomplish what is now being done, the saving of many lives.'

"The pattern," Guruji said, "was not meant to break Joseph. It was meant to shape him."

He fell silent for a moment, then said softly:

"Suffering is not the soul being judged. It is the soul being taught. Joy is not reward. It is in resonance with understanding. When wisdom arrives, repetition leaves—quietly, gratefully—as a teacher who knows the student has finally learned."

And in that silence, Vidyarthi felt something ease—not because the mystery was solved, but because it was finally *understood.*

He looked back at Vidyarthi, his eyes calm, almost amused, as though he were watching a familiar truth arrive again.

Guruji said softly, quoting Rumi:

"One went to the door of the Beloved and knocked.

A voice asked, 'Who is there?'

He answered, 'It is I.'

The voice replied, 'There is no room here for me and thee.'

And the door was shut."

Guruji let the silence linger.

"That first knocking," he said, "was sincere—but it was crowded. The seeker carried himself with him. His longing was real, yet it still said *I want, I seek, I suffer.* Two could not enter where only One exists."

He continued:

"After a year of solitude and burning deprivation, the man returned.

He knocked again.

The voice asked, 'Who is there?'

This time he answered, 'It is Thou.'

And the door was opened."

Guruji's voice lowered, almost to a whisper.

"Nothing about the door changed. Nothing about the Beloved changed. Only the one who knocked was no longer there."

"And the Sufis," he said, a faint smile touching his lips, "tell this story not as poetry alone, but as a map."

He gestured gently, as if tracing an invisible circle in the air.

"The lover keeps returning to the same door. Each rejection feels like punishment. Each silence feels cruel. Yet the door is not closed in anger—it is closed in truth. The Beloved does not reject the lover; the Beloved rejects the *illusion of separation*."

He looked at Vidyarthi steadily.

"The pattern repeats until the 'I' that experiences it dissolves."

"In Sufi wisdom, this is called **fanā**—the annihilation of the ego, the melting of the separate self. The nafs, the false 'I', believes it is knocking toward God. But God is not elsewhere. The very belief that *I am outside* is the wall."

Guruji continued,

"The lover says, 'It is I'—and the door remains shut. Not because love is insufficient, but because *identity is misplaced*. He still believes himself to be a visitor."

He paused.

"After suffering, silence, remembrance, and surrender, something breaks—not the heart, but the boundary. The lover no longer claims authorship of longing. He no longer stands apart from love."

He smiled gently.

"So when the voice asks again, 'Who is there?' the answer comes naturally: 'It is You.'"

"At that moment," Guruji said, "the knocking ceases to be an effort. There is no seeker left to seek, no door left to cross. Entry happens because separation ends."

He leaned forward slightly.

"This is why the door opens. Not because the lover learned better words—but because the *speaker vanished.*"

Guruji's voice softened further.

"This is also why suffering repeats in life. Each repetition is another knock. Each unanswered prayer asks the same question: *Who is there?*"

He held Vidyarthi's gaze.

"As long as the answer is 'It is I—the wounded one, the deserving one, the fearful one'—the pattern continues. Not as punishment, but as invitation."

He said quietly: "The moment the answer becomes, 'Not I, but Thou—not my will, not my story, not my becoming'—the door opens. And one realises it was never locked."

The room felt still—not empty, but full.

Guruji drew another circle, this time breaking it open.

"Across generations, patterns reappear because tendencies travel—fear unhealed becomes inheritance, love unfinished becomes longing. Trauma repeats until it is met with awareness. Compassion repeats until it becomes wisdom. This is not punishment—it is mercy disguised as persistence."

He leaned closer.

"Suffering asks one question: *Have you understood yet?*

Joy asks another: *Can you remain awake here too?*"

Guruji's voice grew still.

"When understanding completes, patterns do not return. They bow and move on."

Vidyarthi lowered his head—not in fear, not in guilt—but in relief.

Aastha asked softly, "Guruji, how can freedom truly unfold when every choice moves within a tapestry already woven by past actions?"

Guruji spoke slowly.

"Child," he said, "this is the oldest question the soul has ever asked—*if the path already exists, why am I asked to walk it?*"

He closed his eyes for a moment, then began with a story.

The River and the Boat

"There is a river," Guruji said, "that flows from the mountains to the sea. Its course is ancient, carved long before you were born. Stones know it. Trees know it. The river cannot suddenly decide to flow uphill. This is destiny—the given framework of experience."

"But on that river," he continued, "floats a small boat. The boat has a rudder. The river decides *where* you will travel; the rudder decides *how* you will travel."

"You may drift gently, or fight the current, or learn its rhythm and move with grace. The river does not cancel your freedom; it gives it a field to operate."

"This," Guruji said softly, "is how choice and consequence coexist."

The Bhagavad Gita: Freedom Within Duty

"In the *Bhagavad Gita*," Guruji said, "Arjuna stands not at the beginning of a story, but in the middle of one already unfolding. The armies are arranged, the conches have sounded, and the weight of history presses upon him. The war is inevitable—its causes lie in choices made long before this moment."

Krishna does not say, *'The war will not happen.'* Nor does He say, *'You are a helpless pawn.'*

Instead, He reveals the heart of freedom within inevitability: *From Bhagavad Gita 2.47* karmany evādhikāras te mā phaleshu kadācana|

ma karma-phala-hetur bhur ma te sango 'stvakarmani||

Meaning: You have the right to perform your prescribed duty, but not to the fruits of action. Do not see yourself as the sole cause of results, and do not fall into attachment to inaction.

Guruji explained, "In this single verse, Krishna offers the complete science of action:

- **Act**—do not escape your responsibility.
- **Release the outcome**—results are shaped by many forces beyond you.
- **Abandon egoic doership**—you are an instrument, not the author of the universe.
- **Avoid paralysis**—renunciation of action is not freedom, it is fear."

"The battlefield," Guruji said softly, "is destiny. Arjuna did not choose the war—but he *does* choose how to stand within it."

"If destiny were absolute, there would be no teaching. If freedom were absolute, there would be no trembling."

"Choice," he said, "exists not to cancel consequence, but to transform bondage into wisdom. This is freedom within duty—the Gita's quiet revolution."

The Upanishads: The Script and the Witness

"The Upanishads go deeper," Guruji said, his voice almost a whisper.

"They say the soul is both **kartā** (the doer) and **sākshi** (the witness)."

'The Self is not born, nor does it die… It is untouched by what the body does.'

(Katha Upanishad 1.2.18)

"Your experiences unfold like a script written by past tendencies—*vasanas*—but your awareness of them is free."

"The story may be written," Guruji said, "but **how consciously you read it changes everything**."

"One who reads blindly is bound.

One who reads with understanding is liberated."

The Puranas: The Weaver's Loom

"In the Puranas," Guruji continued, "karma is compared to a loom."

"The threads are old—woven by past actions. You do not choose the threads you inherit. But you choose **how to weave today**."

"King Bharata inherited a kingdom and immense virtue. His momentary attachment wove another birth—but his awareness in that birth completed the pattern."

"What was written did not imprison him. It educated him."

"Repetition," Guruji said gently, "is not cruelty. It is compassion refusing to abandon an unfinished lesson."

The Bible: The Potter and the Clay

"Even the Bible," Guruji said, "holds this paradox with tenderness."

In Jeremiah, it is written:

'Like clay in the hand of the potter, so are you in My hand.' (Jeremiah 18:6)

"The clay does not choose its moisture or texture—that is destiny. But it can soften or harden under the potter's hands."

"Pharaoh's heart hardened. Joseph's heart softened."

"Both walked into suffering. One became bitter; the other became a blessing to nations."

"The circumstance was given. The response was chosen."

The Sufi Whisper: The Dance Within the Circle

"And the Sufis," Guruji smiled, "say life is a circle already drawn."

"You cannot step outside the circle," he said, "but you may dance within it."

"Some dance with resistance, scraping their feet in complaint. Others whirl until the dancer disappears and only the dance remains."

"When Rumi says, *'Why are you so busy with this or that, good or bad—pay attention to how things blend,'* he is pointing to this truth."

"The framework is fixed. **The intimacy with it is free.**"

The Key That Unlocks the Paradox

Guruji looked directly at Aastha.

"Freedom does not mean choosing what happens.

Freedom means choosing **who you become in what happens**."

"Consequences are in the classroom. Choice is the attitude of the student."

"When understanding dawns, the same karma that once bound becomes the very path of release."

He paused, letting the words sink into the hall.

"Destiny sets the stage.

Free will decides whether the play is a tragedy, comedy, or awakening."

"And liberation," Guruji said softly, "is not escaping the script—but realising you were never only the character. You were also the reader."

The hall fell silent—not with confusion, but with recognition.

Abhirami asked, "Guruji, if some karma is inherited and some is created anew, where does true responsibility begin—and where does the possibility of liberation arise?"

Guruji listened to Abhirami with a stillness that felt like prayer. The hall seemed to soften around her question, as if even the walls understood its weight.

He spoke slowly.

"Responsibility does not begin where karma begins.

It begins where **awareness** begins."

The River and the Oar

"Imagine," Guruji said, "a river flowing from distant mountains. Its current is strong, shaped by rains long past. You did not choose the river—you were born into it. That is **Prarabdha karma**: the body you received, the family, the temperament, the joys and wounds already in motion."

He paused, then lifted his hand gently.

"But the river hands you an oar. That oar is **choice**."

"You cannot stop the current, but you can steer. Responsibility begins the moment you realise you are not the river."

The Gita's Teaching: Action Without Bondage

"In the *Bhagavad Gita chapter 5 Verse 14*," Guruji continued, "Krishna makes a precise distinction."

na kartritvam na **karmāni lokasya srijati prabhuh**

na karma-phala-saṁyogaṁ svabhāvas tu pravartate

Meaning: The Divine does not create doership, actions, or the connection between action and result. These arise from nature itself.

"Do you hear it?" Guruji asked softly.

"Action happens through nature. Bondage happens through **identification**."

"Karma binds only when you say, *'I am the doer.'*

Liberation begins when you say, *'Action happens through me, but I am not confined to it.'*"

The Upanishadic Shift: From Actor to Witness

"The *Upanishads* go further," Guruji said, his voice gentle yet precise.

dvā suparnā sayujā sakhāyā
samānaṁ vrksaṁ parisasvajāte
tayor anyah pippalaṁ svādv atty
anasnann anyo 'bhicākasīti
(Muṇḍaka Upaniṣad 3.1.1)

Meaning:

Two birds, united companions, perch upon the same tree.

One bird eats the fruit of the tree—sweet and bitter.

The other does not eat; it only watches.

Guruji paused, letting the image settle.

"The tree is the body.

The fruits are experiences—pleasure and pain, success and loss.

The eating bird is the **doer**, entangled in consequence.

The watching bird is the **witness**, untouched and free."

He continued softly:

"Responsibility belongs to the bird that eats—

for it chooses, reacts, and tastes the world."

"But liberation belongs to the bird that remembers—

the silent seer who was never bound by the flavour of events."

"When awareness shifts from **experience** to the **experiencer**,
karma does not disappear—

but its power to bind dissolves."

"The Upanishads do not ask you to stop living. They ask you to remember *who is truly living through you.*"

The hall grew still—not with tension, but with recognition.

A Puranic Story: The Archer and the Wind

Guruji shared a story.

"A young archer once blamed the wind for missing his target. His teacher said, 'The wind chooses the direction of the arrow's drift—but you chose where to aim.'"

"Past karma is the wind.

Present awareness is the aim."

"You are not responsible for the wind—but you are responsible for consciousness."

The Bible: Freedom Within Inheritance

"Even the Bible understands this," Guruji said.

Saint Paul writes:

'For I do not do the good I want to do, but the evil I do not want to do—this I keep on doing.'

(Romans 7:19)

"This is not a confession of guilt—it is a recognition of conditioning."

"But Paul does not stop there."

'Where the Spirit of the Lord is, there is freedom.'

(2 Corinthians 3:17)

"Freedom does not erase inheritance—it **transcends** it."

The Sufi Mirror: Where Responsibility Meets Surrender

Guruji smiled faintly, as though remembering something ancient.

"In the Sufi tradition," he said, "there is a well-known *Hadith* on **tawakkul**—true trust."

A man once asked the Prophet Muhammad (peace be upon him),

"Should I tie my camel and trust in God, or leave it untied and trust in God?"

The Prophet replied,

"Tie your camel—and then trust in God."

Guruji let the words breathe.

"Tying the camel is a **responsibility**.

Trusting God is **liberation**."

"One without the other is incomplete.

Action without surrender becomes anxiety.

Surrender without action becomes avoidance."

He continued softly:

"Do what awareness asks of you—clearly, sincerely, fully.
Then release the demand to control the outcome."

"When the 'I' that clings to results dissolves,

karma does not disappear—

but it no longer has an owner."

"In that moment," Guruji said, "action continues, consequences unfold, yet the soul stands free—acting without bondage, trusting without fear."

Where Responsibility Begins, Where Liberation Flowers

Guruji looked directly at Abhirami.

"Responsibility begins the moment you realise you are not helpless.

Liberation becomes possible the moment you realise you are not the doer."

"Karma continues—but it no longer binds.

The river still flows—but you are no longer drowning in it."

He said softly:

"You are answerable for **how consciously you live**, not for the conditions you inherited.

And liberation is not the absence of karma—it is the absence of *attachment to being its prisoner.*"

The hall fell silent—not heavy, but luminous.

Guruji paused, as though listening to something only silence could say. Then, without ceremony, he rose from his āsana and walked out of the Buddha Hall. No final words were spoken. None were needed. The day's teachings had already settled like seeds into waiting soil.

One by one, the devotees followed, their footsteps soft, their minds full. Soon the Buddha Hall stood empty of human presence—yet it did not feel vacant. The space retained a warmth, as if the air itself remembered Guruji's stillness. Lamps flickered gently along the walls, shadows stretching and dissolving.

Outside, the sky had deepened into a vast indigo, scattered with stars that blinked patiently through drifting clouds, as though playing an ancient game of hide-and-seek with the moon.

The wind moved quietly through the courtyards, rustling leaves like pages being turned. Frogs began their nocturnal hymns by the water's edge, insects added their steady drone, and night birds called out from unseen branches. It felt as though the world itself had gathered to continue the discourse—in another language, softer and more inclusive. Even silence, here, was alive.

Drawn by hunger and companionship, the devotees made their way toward the food centre. Dinner was simple, nourishing, and unhurried. No one spoke much at first. The teachings were still digesting.

Later, beneath the open sky, Vidyarthi, Aastha, Akshaya, Kiran, Padma, Vasudeva, and Abhirami gathered around a small fireplace. The flames licked the cool night air, crackling gently, throwing moving shadows across their faces. The warmth was immediate—not just of fire, but of shared presence. Words began to flow naturally: reflections on karma and choice, quiet confessions of struggle, laughter over human frailty, and reverent pauses when Guruji's insights resurfaced between sentences.

Gradually, more devotees arrived, as if drawn by an unseen signal. Bhavya, Aarna, Dev, Kiran, Sam, Alice, Sofia, and John joined the circle, their voices carrying the lightness of a short evening walk. Soon after came Nita, Lalitha, Rohith, and Sujitha, adding new rhythms to the conversation—some listening deeply, others speaking with animated gestures, all held by the same shared intent.

Moments later, Akshatha, Apeksha, Abhilasha, Akanksh, and Roopa appeared, their eyes still glowing with contemplation. Behind them followed Kieron, Astyn, Espen, Greta, and Divyani, bringing with them the quiet hum of curiosity shaped by different lands, different lives, yet the same inward hunger.

As the circle widened, the fire burned steadier.

Then Akshatha's voice rose—calm, playful, and expectant.

"Time for Apeksha's story…"

Apeksha inhaled slowly, her gaze resting briefly on the flames, as if gathering courage not from words but from the silence between them. And then she began to speak.

The Weaver and the Half-Finished Cloth

The fire crackled softly as Apeksha lifted her gaze. For a moment, she said nothing, as if listening inward. Then she began.

"Once, in a small village near a river, there lived an old weaver," she said.

"He was known for his skill, yet every cloth he wove carried a strange flaw—one corner was always unfinished."

The villagers noticed it. Some whispered that he lacked discipline. Others said age had made his hands unsteady. Yet kings still came, because something in his clothes felt alive.

One evening, a young apprentice finally asked,

"Master, why do you leave every cloth incomplete?"

The weaver smiled and led him to a pile of unfinished fabrics stacked in the corner.

"Each of these," he said, "belongs to a season of my life."

As a young man, the weaver had rushed his work, driven by hunger.

As a father, he wove while worrying about his children.

As a grieving husband, his hands trembled with loss.

"Every time my life changed," the weaver said softly,

"I had to stop. Not because the cloth was wrong—but because *I* was unfinished."

The apprentice frowned.

"Then why not complete them now?"

The old man touched the loom gently.

"Because the cloth is not waiting for my hands.

It is waiting for my understanding."

He looked toward the river, its water flowing endlessly yet never repeating itself.

"Life," he continued, "does not punish us with repetition.

It returns us to what we left half-seen."

That night, after the weaver died, the apprentice tried finishing one cloth.

But no matter how carefully he wove, the fabric lost its quiet power.

Only later did he understand:

the missing thread was not skill—it was *consciousness*.

Apeksha's voice softened.

"Karma," she said,

"is not a sentence handed down.

It is a lesson paused mid-breath."

"We return—not because we failed—but because we are capable of deeper seeing."

The fire popped, sending a brief spray of sparks upward, like questions rising into the night.

"When understanding completes the pattern," Apeksha said, "the loom falls silent.

Not because work is finished— but because the weaver has remembered who he is."

Silence followed—not empty, but full.

No one spoke for a while.

The night seemed to lean closer, as if listening.

The fire crackled. The stars watched.

One by one, as the night deepened, the devotees rose. There was no rush. Movements were soft, mindful, like leaves carried by a knowing wind. Paths diverged toward individual chambers, yet something invisible bound them together still. The lessons of the day walked with them—not as thoughts, but as quiet companions.

The fire was left with glowing embers, breathing gently into the dark.

And thus, the night in Kanchipuram became more than a night. It became a sanctuary—a bridge between what had been understood and what was yet to unfold. A reminder that learning does not end with words, nor wisdom with daylight. Even in stillness, life continued to teach—patiently, subtly, as constant as the stars above and the quiet knowing within.

PART TWO

THE SACRED PREPARATION

The soul does not rush into birth

"Every moment you feel incomplete is the universe gently reminding you of a promise you once accepted."

- *Shree Shambav*

CHAPTER IV

Stage One

The Call of Universal Consciousness

"Longing is not a wound—it is the soul remembering that it came to become."

– Shree Shambav.

Synopsis

This chapter unfolds in a sacred stillness, where silence, light, and waiting hearts prepare the ground for a deeper revelation. As the teacher begins to speak, the reader is guided into a contemplative space where time itself seems to pause, allowing a truth older than memory to surface gently.

At its core, the chapter explores The Sacred Preparation*—the mysterious moment before birth, when the soul does not rush into life but chooses it. Incarnation is revealed not as compulsion or consequence, but as a conscious movement of love. Through poetic* *reflection and the story of a flame that longs to know itself through illumination, the chapter explains how longing arises not from lack, but from fullness seeking expression.*

Human restlessness, dissatisfaction, and the ache for meaning are reframed as sacred echoes of this original choice. Limitation is no longer punishment, but a teacher embraced by the soul. The chapter invites readers to recognise their own yearning as remembrance—a quiet call from within, inviting them to encounter eternity through the fragile beauty of lived experience.

The morning in **Kanchipuram** unfolded like a quiet hymn to existence itself. Dawn arrived gently, its first light brushing the ancient temple towers, crowning their golden tips with a softness that felt almost reverent. The air remained cool, still carrying the fragrance of jasmine and parijata blossoms that had fallen during the night, as though the earth itself had offered prayers in sleep.

Birdsong rose slowly, not as noise but as invocation—calling the soul awake before the body stirred. Along the garden paths surrounding **Buddha Hall**, devotees walked unhurriedly. Some moved in silence, others with folded palms, each step reflecting a heart that had emptied itself in the night and now returned, quietly yearning for light.

Inside the hall, oil lamps still flickered from the vigil that had carried them through darkness. Their flames trembled softly, casting gentle shadows upon the walls. The lingering scent of sandalwood mingled with the stillness of morning, creating a space that felt neither night nor day, but a threshold between worlds.

The devotees took their places. Some closed their eyes in wordless prayer; others gazed steadily at the empty seat where **Guruji** would soon sit—waiting not just for his arrival, but for remembrance.

When he entered, the peace he carried seemed to harmonise effortlessly with the hour. His smile mirrored the calm of the morning sky. He walked with measured grace, each step itself a silent teaching. As he took his seat, he closed his eyes, hands resting lightly upon his knees.

The hall grew utterly still—so still it felt as though time itself had paused, bowing in quiet reverence.

After a moment that felt both fleeting and eternal, Guruji opened his eyes. When he spoke, his voice was soft yet resonant, like a temple bell whose sound does not merely fill the air but settles deep within the heart.

THE SACRED PREPARATION

When Eternity Chooses to Touch Time

Guruji's voice was calm, but something vast moved behind it.

"The soul does not rush into birth—it prepares."

Before time begins to count itself in days and years, before form takes a name or memory claims an identity, there is a pause in eternity. A stillness so complete that even wholeness becomes aware of itself. Nothing is missing. Nothing is broken. And yet—something stirs.

Not as hunger.

Not as desire.

But as a **possibility**.

Guruji said softly, "In the depths of Universal Consciousness, there arises a quiet stirring. A sacred dissatisfaction—not born of lack, but of fullness yearning to be expressed."

This is **Stage One: The Call of Universal Consciousness**.

It is not a command issued by fate.

It is not a debt owed to karma.

It is an invitation whispered by love itself.

The First Stirring

In the Chandogya Upanishad (6.2.3) and also in the Aitareya Upanishad, creation begins with a startlingly intimate declaration:

"Bahusyam prajāyeya" — *Let me become many. Let me enter into forms.*"

Not because the One was incomplete, but because completeness wished to be **experienced**.

Guruji continued,

"Before identity becomes 'I am this,' consciousness rests as 'I am.' In that resting, awareness senses a question—not spoken, but felt: *What is it like to know myself through relationship, resistance, reflection?*"

This is the soul's first listening.

The Story of the Flame

Guruji paused, then said, "Let me narrate a story."

Imagine a flame that has always known itself only as light.
It has never known darkness.

Never met resistance.

Never seen its glow reflected in another's eyes.

One day—not in time, but in awareness—the flame wonders:

What is it like to illuminate something other than myself?

That wondering is not weakness.

It is **creative courage**.

To shine upon form, the flame must accept shadow.

To reveal colour, it must meet limitations.

To know itself as warmth, it must touch what is cold.

"That wondering," Guruji said, "is the beginning of incarnation."

The soul, resting in Universal Consciousness, feels a gentle ache.

Not pain—but **possibility**.

Like silence before music.

Like breath before speech.

Like the pause before love says its own name.

Sacred Dissatisfaction

Guruji's voice deepened.

"This dissatisfaction is sacred. It is not the soul rejecting wholeness—it is wholeness seeking expression."

The Bhagavad Gita hints at this mystery when Krishna speaks of the eternal Self entering the field of prakriti, not because it is bound, but because it **chooses to engage**:

"Though unborn and imperishable, I appear in the world through my own power." (Gita 4.6)

Incarnation begins not with fall, but with **choice**.

The soul knows:

To enter the form is to forget.

To forget is to struggle.

To struggle is to grow.

To grow is to remember—more deeply than before.

Why Longing Exists

Guruji said, "Longing is not a flaw. It is the echo of the soul's first 'yes.'"

In the human heart, this echo appears as restlessness.

As the feeling that something is missing—even when life looks complete.

As love that seeks depth, truth that seeks meaning, beauty that seeks eternity.

The Sufis say, *"I was a hidden treasure, and I loved to be known."*

So the Beloved hid—

not out of fear,

but out of love for the seeker's joy.

Likewise, the soul enters form not to escape eternity, but to **encounter it from within time**.

Limitation as Teacher

Guruji said, "Limitation is not punishment. It is curriculum."

In the Puranas, Vishnu descends again and again—not because he is bound, but because relationship teaches what abstraction cannot. Rama learns duty through exile. Krishna learns love through play. Each descent is a lesson chosen, not imposed.

Even the Bible echoes this mystery:

"The Word became flesh and dwelt among us." (John 1:14)

Not because the Word lacked power—

but because love desires **closeness**.

The Human Echo

Guruji looked around the hall.

"What the soul experiences before birth, humans experience in life."

Your longing to create.

Your ache for meaning.

Your dissatisfaction with surface success.

Your quiet feeling that life must be more than survival.

These are not problems to be solved.

They are **reminders**.

"Human restlessness mirrors the soul's original invitation."

You are not broken.

You are remembering.

Guruji said:

- Longing arises not from lack, but from the urge to express fullness
- Incarnation begins with choice, not compulsion
- Limitation is embraced as a sacred teacher

- Human yearning echoes the soul's first call toward experience

He asked gently,

"Why does longing exist in the eternal?

Is incarnation optional?

Why does the soul desire limitation?

And how does this ancient call echo through your own life—right now?"

The hall remained silent.

Not empty.

Listening.

Kieron asked, "Guruji, if the soul is already complete, what kind of longing arises—not from lack, but from the fullness of being?"

Guruji's eyes softened, not as one answering a question, but as one remembering something ancient.

He said gently, "Kieron, we have been taught to believe that longing is born only from emptiness. But this is the language of survival, not of the soul."

He paused, then began.

The Paradox of Fullness

"Tell me," Guruji asked, "does a river flow because it is empty—or because it is full?"

A river does not rush toward the ocean out of poverty. It flows because its fullness has nowhere else to go. The mountain does not give birth to the river because it lacks water, but because abundance seeks movement.

"So it is with the soul," Guruji said. "Its longing is not a wound. It is an overflow."

In the Upanishads, creation does not begin with need, but with wonder:

'Let me become many.'

Not because the One was incomplete—but because completeness wished to be known through reflection.

The Story of the Lamp

Guruji said, "Let me narrate a story. Imagine a lamp burning alone in an endless room. The flame is steady, perfect, self-sufficient. It needs nothing. Yet one evening, a mirror is placed before it.

For the first time, the flame sees itself shining *elsewhere*.

A strange tenderness arises—not lack, not desire—but curiosity.

The flame thinks, *What is it like to be seen? What is it like to illuminate another?*"

Guruji smiled.

"That curiosity is longing born of fullness. The lamp did not suffer before the mirror arrived. But after reflection, a new dimension of joy became possible."

Longing as Love in Motion

"In the Bhagavad Gita," Guruji continued, "Krishna says that though unborn and eternal, he enters the world by his own will."

Love that is complete does not remain still forever. It moves—not because it must, but because it can.

The Puranas speak of the divine playing, descending, returning—not out of bondage, but delight.

The Bible echoes the same mystery when it says: *'The Word became flesh.'*

Not because the Word was weak—but because love desires nearness.

The Sufis say it most nakedly:

"I was a hidden treasure, and I loved to be known."

Guruji looked at Kieron.

"Notice the word: loved. Not needed."

Why the Human Heart Feels Restless

"Your restlessness," Guruji said softly, "is not proof that something is missing. It is proof that something vast lives within you."

A child who has learned one song longs to sing another—not because the first was insufficient, but because joy expands through expression.

An artist finishes a painting and immediately reaches for another canvas—not from dissatisfaction, but from creative abundance.

Likewise, the soul—whole and luminous—chooses experience so it may *taste* itself.

"To know peace is one thing," Guruji said.

"To choose peace amid noise is another."

"To know love in eternity is one thing.

"To love through separation, risk, and return is deeper knowing."

The Final Turning

Guruji said:

"Longing from absence says, *I am not enough.*

Longing from fullness says, *I am so much that I must move.*"

The first binds.

The second creates.

"So when longing arises in you," he said, "do not ask, *What am I missing?*

Ask instead, *What wants to be expressed through me?*"

The hall was silent.

Not because the answer was complete—

but because something within had recognised itself.

Astyn asked, "Guruji, if incarnation is a choice, what does this reveal about the nature of fate and the responsibility we carry in life?"

Astyn's question did not fall into the hall like a query—it arrived like a bell whose echo lingered even before it was struck.

Guruji remained silent for a long moment. Not because the answer was distant, but because it was intimate.

Then he spoke.

The Difference Between Being Sent and Choosing to Come

"Astyn," Guruji said softly, "to believe that incarnation is a punishment is to misunderstand love. To believe it is an accident is to misunderstand intelligence."

He leaned forward slightly.

"Incarnation is not exile. It is participation."

Most people imagine birth as something that *happens* to the soul—pushed by karma, dragged by desire, trapped by unfinished business. But the wisdom traditions whisper something far more radical:

The soul consents.

In the Bhagavad Gita, Krishna does not say, *I am forced into the world.*

He says, "Though unborn and imperishable, I appear by My own power." (4.6)

"Choice," Guruji said, "is the signature of consciousness."

The Story of the Musician

"Let me tell you a story."

Imagine a master musician who has heard all sounds within himself. Every note, every harmony, every silence already exists in his knowing. He lacks nothing.

Yet one evening, he lifts an instrument.

The strings resist his fingers.

The air vibrates imperfectly.

The audience coughs, shifts, and misunderstands.

Why would a master enter limitation?

Because **music is not meant only to be known—it is meant to be played.**

Guruji smiled.

"The soul incarnates for the same reason. Eternity knows itself. Time lets it *experience* itself."

Choice Transforms Karma

"If incarnation is chosen," Guruji continued, "karma is no longer a prison. It becomes a classroom."

The Puranas speak of divine descents not as entrapments, but as *leelas*—sacred play. Vishnu does not fall into the world; he enters it. Rama accepts exile. Krishna accepts birth among cowherds.

Each form carries a constraint.

Each constraint carries a lesson.

Each lesson was agreed upon before the curtain rose.

The Upanishads say the Self enters the body as a king enters a city—not as a captive, but as a witness who forgets, so remembering can be meaningful.

"Forgetfulness," Guruji said, "is not failure. It is part of the design."

The Cross and the Descent

The Bible echoes this mystery when it speaks of the Word becoming flesh.

Not dragged.

Not diminished.

But *dwelling among.*

Love does not remain distant. It steps closer—even when closeness risks pain.

Guruji said, "The cross is not merely suffering—it is consent. Love saying, *I will not stay untouched.*"

The Sufis understand this well. They say the Beloved veils itself, not to escape, but so the seeker may taste longing, devotion, return.

"Without veiling," Guruji said, "there is no intimacy."

What This Changes for You

Guruji looked around the hall.

"If incarnation is a choice," he said, "then your life is not a sentence. It is a syllabus."

Your challenges are not cosmic mistakes.

Your limits are not evidence of abandonment.

Your pain is not proof of unworthiness.

They are **selected conditions**—not consciously remembered, but deeply known.

"When you see life this way," Guruji continued,

"victimhood dissolves. Responsibility awakens."

Not blame.

Not guilt.

But authorship.

The Quiet Revolution

Guruji said:

"If you chose to be here, then meaning is not something you chase—it is something you uncover."

You stop asking, *Why is this happening to me?*

You begin asking, *What is this shaping in me?*

Incarnation as choice transforms suffering into initiation, limitation into curriculum, and life into a sacred dialogue between eternity and time.

He paused, then asked gently:

"If you came by choice…

what kind of courage must your soul possess?"

The silence that followed was not heavy.

It was awake.

Greta asked, "Guruji, why would an eternal being choose to enter limitation, forgetting, and suffering as part of its journey?"

Greta's question did not sound like curiosity alone—it carried the ache of every human heart that has ever wondered whether pain has meaning.

Guruji closed his eyes for a moment, as though listening not to thought, but to something older than words. When he spoke, his voice was gentle, almost tender.

The Courage to Become Small

"Greta," he said softly, "only that which is infinite can afford to become finite."

He let the silence breathe.

"Limitation is not imposed on the eternal. It is *chosen*—not because the Eternal is weak, but because it is fearless."

We imagine perfection as something that must remain untouched, sealed away from struggle. But the great traditions tell a different story: **true fullness is not afraid of loss, because it knows it cannot truly be diminished.**

Guruji explained, "Power is not only the ability to rule. It is the ability to enter vulnerability without losing one's essence."

The Story of the Ocean and the Wave

"Let me tell you a story," Guruji said.

Imagine an infinite ocean—vast, silent, complete. Nothing threatens it. Nothing limits it.

One day, the ocean wonders:

What is it like to dance?

So it becomes a wave.

The wave rises—exhilaration.

The wave crashes—pain.

The wave dissolves—loss.

But the ocean was never harmed.

"Pain," Guruji said, "belongs to the wave. Freedom belongs to the ocean. Yet without the wave, the ocean would never know movement."

A limitation is the price of experience. Experience is the doorway to intimacy.

Forgetting as Sacred Design

Greta listened closely as Guruji continued.

"The Upanishads say the Self enters the body and forgets itself. Not as punishment—but as necessity."

Why forget?

Because remembrance without forgetting is shallow.

Like reading the answer without living the question.

The Mundaka Upanishad gives the image of two birds on one tree—one eats the fruit, the other watches. The eating bird forgets its true nature. The watching bird remembers.

"Liberation," Guruji said, "is not escape from the tree. It is remembering who you are while sitting on it."

Pain as the Teacher of Depth

"In the Puranas," Guruji continued, "the higher divine energies descend again and again—not to suffer needlessly, but to *learn relationship*."

Rama learns duty through exile.

Krishna learns love through separation.

Shiva learns compassion through loss.

Pain carves depth where comfort cannot.

Even the Bible echoes this mystery:

'Though He was divine, He emptied Himself and took the form of a servant.' (Philippians 2:7)

Guruji said, "Love does not remain abstract. It risks embodiment."

The Sufi Secret

The Sufis say: *'I was a hidden treasure, and I loved to be known.'*

To be known, the Beloved must hide.

To be sought, the Beloved must withdraw.

To be loved, the Beloved must risk rejection.

"Pain," Guruji said, "is not the opposite of love. It is love's shadow when love enters time."

Why the Eternal Accepts Pain

Guruji looked at Greta with quiet compassion.

"The eternal accepts pain not because it is necessary—but because it is meaningful."

Without pain:

- Courage would have no test
- Compassion would have no depth
- Forgiveness would have no cost

- Love would have no proof

"Pain," he said, "is the friction that turns potential into wisdom."

What This Means for You

"If the eternal could accept limitation," Guruji said, "then your suffering is not a mistake. It is a passage."

You are not broken because you hurt.

You are not abandoned because you forget.

You are not weak because you struggle.

You are participating in a cosmic courage—the bravery of consciousness choosing to *feel.*

He asked softly:

"If eternity trusted you enough to carry its forgetting…

what might it also trust you to remember?"

The hall was silent again.

Not silent with sorrow.

Silent with reverence.

Espen asked, "Guruji, how does this primordial call continue to stir within us, manifesting as restlessness, creativity, or the sense that something greater awaits?"

Espen's question lingered in the hall like a bell whose sound had not yet finished ringing. It was not philosophical curiosity alone—it was the quiet confession of every human heart that has achieved much, loved deeply, and yet still feels an unnamed pull toward *something more.*

Guruji looked at him with gentle recognition.

"Yes," he said softly, "that feeling has a very ancient origin."

The Echo That Never Stopped

"The primordial call does not end with incarnation," Guruji began.

"It echoes *through* incarnation."

What the soul once felt as a sacred stirring in eternity, the human being feels as restlessness in time.

Not because life is insufficient—

but because life remembers its origin.

The Hidden Pull of Nature

In the **Bhagavad Gita (3.33)**, Krishna reveals a truth that is both unsettling and liberating:

sadrisham cheshtate svasyah prakriter jnanavan api |

prakritim yanti bhutani nigrahah kim karishyati | |

Meaning: Even the wise act according to their own nature, for all beings follow their inherent tendencies. What can repression accomplish?

Guruji explained softly, "Krishna is saying something radical here. Even wisdom does not erase nature's pull. Even insight does not cancel the momentum already in motion."

There is something **older than logic**, deeper than decision-making—a primordial current carrying consciousness forward through *prakṛti.* Something within us moves **before thought**, before reasoning has time to assemble its arguments.

"This movement," Guruji said, "is not weakness. It is the echo of the soul's deeper intention unfolding through nature."

After a pause, he added another verse, sharpening the insight:

Bhagavad Gita (18.60)

svabhāvajena kaunteya nibaddhah svena karmanā |

kartuṁ necchasi yan mohāt karisyasy avaśo’pi tat ||

Meaning: O Arjuna, bound by your own nature and past actions, you will act—even against your will—driven as though helpless.

Krishna is not denying free will here. He is revealing **why restlessness persists even when we resist it**.

What moves us is not mere habit or impulse. It is **unfinished understanding seeking expression**.

Guruji said quietly, “This movement is memory without images. A remembrance without words.”

- The soul carries a momentum older than thought
- Nature expresses what consciousness has not yet completed
- Resistance drives this force underground; understanding brings it into light
- Awareness transforms compulsion into conscious participation

Krishna is not saying, *“You are trapped.”*

He is saying, *“Know what is moving you—and you will be free.”*

Freedom does not begin by stopping the river.

It begins by understanding where it flows—and why.

The Upanishadic Undercurrent: Samskara and Vasana

Guruji said softly, "What Krishna calls *prakrti* in the Gita, the Upanishads call *samskara* and *vasana*—the subtle impressions carried within consciousness itself."

Samskara are not memories stored in the brain. They are **grooves in awareness**, carved by experience across lifetimes.

Vasana is the *fragrance* of those grooves—the tendencies that rise uninvited, shaping desire, fear, creativity, and restlessness before thought intervenes.

In the **Brhadaranyaka Upanishad (4.4.5)** it is said:

"As one acts, so one becomes.

As one desires, so one wills.

As one wills, so one acts."

Guruji explained, "This is not moral judgment—it is continuity. Consciousness moves along the pathways it has already traced. Even the wise feel these movements, because wisdom does not erase momentum—it illuminates it."

Why Something Moves Before Thought

"When intuition speaks without logic," Guruji said, "it is not the mind inventing—it is **vasana** seeking completion."

This is why creativity arrives unannounced.

Why longing appears without explanation.

Why resistance often intensifies the very impulse we try to suppress.

Something within us moves **before thought**, before reasoning gathers its arguments. The mind explains later; the movement begins earlier.

The **Katha Upanishad (2.3.14)** points directly to this hidden engine of life:

yadā sarve pramucyante kāmā ye'sya hrdi sritāh

atha martyo'mrto bhavatyatra brahma samasnute

Meaning: When all the desires that have taken root in the heart are fully released, the mortal becomes immortal; here and now, one attains Brahman.

Guruji explained gently, "This verse does not condemn desire. It reveals its **completion**."

"Desires do not fall away because they are crushed. They fall away because their deeper purpose has been understood. When the heart no longer seeks wholeness outside itself, the sense of mortality loosens its grip."

He paused, letting the words settle.

"The Upanishad does not promise liberation elsewhere, or in some distant future. It says *atra*—**here**. Immortality is not escape from life, but recognition of what has always been alive beneath longing."

Desire gives rise to action.

Action gives rise to consequence.

But desire, Guruji clarified, is not merely craving.

"**Kama**, at its root, means direction," he said. "It is consciousness leaning toward what it has not yet fully seen."

"When intuition stirs, the soul is not demanding pleasure—it is seeking clarity. What moves before thought is not weakness; it is unfinished understanding calling for awareness."

He smiled softly.

"When those understanding dawns, movement does not stop—but bondage does."

Restlessness as Sacred Momentum

"What humans call restlessness," Guruji said quietly, "is often the echo of unresolved **samskara**."

A musician feels an unexplainable pull toward sound.

A seeker is drawn again and again toward silence.

A lover longs not merely for presence, but for union.

These movements are not random desires, nor habits formed in a single lifetime. They are **vasanas**—deep impressions carried by consciousness—ripening, asking to be seen, understood, and fulfilled at the level of awareness.

"This is why restlessness persists," Guruji explained. "Not because something is wrong, but because something within you remembers its own direction."

Krishna speaks directly to this truth in the **Bhagavad Gita (3.33)**:

sadrisham cheshtate svasyah prakriter jnanavan api |

prakritim yanti bhutani nigrahah kim karishyati | |

Meaning: Even the wise act according to their own nature, for all beings follow their inherent tendencies. What can repression accomplish?

"Nature moves first," Guruji said. "Thought follows later."

We see this everywhere.

Ants gather tirelessly, serving the whole before the self.

A cow trembles with unease when her calf disappears from sight.

A dog remains loyal beyond reason, beyond reward.

These beings do not debate their nature. They live it.

"Human beings are no different," Guruji said softly. "We, too, are propelled by inner patterns—but unlike animals, we try to suppress them instead of understanding them."

He paused, letting the fire crackle between his words.

"Suppression does not erase a samskara," he continued. "It only pushes it into the shadows. Awareness allows it to surface, speak, and complete itself."

"When a pattern is seen clearly, it no longer needs to repeat. When a longing is understood, it no longer demands obedience."

Guruji smiled gently.

"Freedom does not come from fighting your nature. It comes from seeing through it."

From Bondage to Liberation

"When samskara remains unconscious, it binds.

When it is seen clearly, it releases."

The **Mundaka Upanishad (2.2.8)** affirms:

bhidyate hrdayagranthischidyante sarvasamsayāh |

ksīyante cāsya karmāni tasmindrste parāvare | |

Meaning: When he that is both high and low is seen, the knot of the heart is untied; all doubts are solved; and all his *karma* is consumed.

Guruji said, "When the knots of the heart are cut, the mortal becomes immortal."

Guruji explained, "The knot is not action—it is ignorance of why the action arises. Liberation does not come by stopping movement, but by seeing its source."

At that moment, vasana loses its compulsive force. What once pushed now gently guides. What once bound now becomes wisdom.

Guruji said, "The soul is never driven blindly. It moves with intelligence older than thought. Samskara is memory without images. Vasana is remembrance without words. Freedom is not the absence of these forces—but the awareness that allows them to fulfil themselves."

"That movement is memory without images. A remembrance without words."

The Story of the Caged Bird

"Let me tell you a story," Guruji said.

A bird is born in a vast sky. It knows flight, wind, and horizon.
One day, it is gently placed in a golden cage—safe, fed, protected.

The bird is not starving.

The cage is not cruel.

And yet, every morning, the bird sings toward the sky.

Why?

Not because the cage is painful—but because the sky is remembered.

"That song," Guruji said, "is restlessness."

Human restlessness is not dissatisfaction with life.

It is nostalgia for infinity.

Creativity as Sacred Leakage

Guruji continued, "When the infinite enters the finite, some of it always leaks through."

That leakage is creativity.

Why do humans paint what cannot be captured? Why do poets write about what cannot be said? Why does music move us to tears without explanation?

The Upanishads say that the Self is *ananda*—creative bliss itself. When that bliss is compressed into form, it seeks expression.

"Creativity," Guruji said, "is eternity tapping on the walls of time."

A dancer remembers freedom through movement. A sculptor remembers silence through stone. A seeker remembers truth through questions.

The Unfinished Sentence

Espen listened as Guruji leaned forward slightly.

"Have you noticed," he asked, "that even joy feels unfinished?"

The Bible speaks of this as holy longing: **Romans 8:23**

'We groan inwardly, waiting for fullness.'

Not groaning from despair—but from anticipation.

The human heart feels like a sentence that ends with ellipses…

That ellipsis is the soul remembering it was once whole *before* it became a story.

The Sufi Candle

The Sufis tell of a candle that burns all night, knowing it will vanish by dawn.

Why does it burn?

Because the flame remembers the sun.

"Your longing," Guruji said, "is not proof that something is missing. It is proof that something infinite once knew itself through you."

The Beloved calls, not loudly—but persistently.

Through beauty.

Through love.

Through loss.

Through the sense that no achievement quite completes the heart.

Why 'Something More' Persists

Guruji said gently:

- Restlessness is the soul remembering motion
- Creativity is the soul remembering expression
- Dissatisfaction is the soul remembering infinity
- The sense of 'something more' is the soul remembering home

"What you call 'more,'" Guruji said, "is not elsewhere. It is deeper."

The Invitation Hidden in Daily Life

"Do not silence restlessness too quickly," he cautioned.
"And do not mistake it for ingratitude."

When honoured, restlessness becomes inquiry.

When resisted, it becomes anxiety.

When understood, it becomes devotion.

Krishna does not tell Arjuna to escape the world—He teaches him to *meet the eternal through action.*

"Life," Guruji said, "is the echo chamber of eternity."

He looked at Espen and asked quietly:

"When restlessness arises in you—

do you rush to fill it…

or do you listen for what is calling?"

The silence that followed was not uneasy.

It was attentive.

As though something ancient had just been recognised again.

CHAPTER V

Stage Two

The Great Life Review

"The soul does not learn through judgment—it learns through resonance."

– Shree Shambav.

Synopsis

This chapter unfolds in the stillness of the Buddha Hall, where Guruji introduces Stage Two: The Great Life Review—a sacred pause between lives. Here, the soul enters a luminous chamber of awareness, not to be judged, but to feel. Free from accusation or authority, the soul relives its past not as memory, but as direct experience—pain inflicted is felt as pain received, love given as expansion returned.

Through a moving parable of a river of light, Guruji reveals that this review is not punishment but resonance. Every action becomes understanding, every mistake a lesson completed through empathy. Guilt dissolves because there is no enemy—only truth embraced fully.

Drawing from the Bhagavad Gita, Upanishads, Puranas, Tibetan Bardo teachings, and mystical traditions across cultures, the chapter emphasises that awareness, not fear, reshapes destiny. By feeling all it once caused, the soul transforms unconscious karma into conscious choice, preparing for rebirth with clarity, compassion, and freedom rather than repetition.

Stage Two: The Great Life Review

Where the Soul Learns by Feeling

The Buddha Hall rested in a luminous hush. Afternoon light poured gently through the high windows, catching dust motes in its glow, each one floating like a small, waiting possibility. After the midday meal and a quiet hour of rest, the devotees returned—unhurried, softened, inwardly open. The hall filled not with sound, but with presence.

After a few moments, Guruji entered and took his asana. Silence settled—not imposed, but invited. His gaze moved slowly across the faces before him, as though listening to something beyond words. When he finally spoke, his voice carried a depth that felt older than memory.

"This," he said gently, "is the moment many traditions speak of—but few truly understand."

The Pause Between Lives

"After answering the call to return into form," Guruji continued, "the soul does not rush forward. It pauses."

He turned slightly toward Nita.

"There is a vast chamber of awareness—not a place, but a state. Silent. Luminous. Utterly honest. No judge sits there. No ledger is opened. No sentence is passed."

"This is not a courtroom," he said softly.

"It is a sanctuary of understanding."

Here, the soul stands alone—yet intimately connected to every life it has touched. Time loosens. Moments once buried rise again, not as memories replayed, but as experiences *entered.*

"The soul does not review life as a witness," Guruji said.

"It reviews life as a *feeler.*"

The River of Light

Then he smiled gently.

"Let me tell you a story."

"Imagine," he said, "a river made entirely of light. Its current is gentle, yet irresistible. Every ripple carries a moment from a life once lived."

As the soul steps into this river, it does not *watch* the past—it becomes it.

A harsh word spoken long ago returns—not as sound, but as a tightening in another's chest.

A betrayal resurfaces—not as shame, but as the ache of abandonment felt in another's bones.

A moment of indifference appears—not as accusation, but as the quiet loneliness of someone unseen.

Then come the other currents.

A hand held in grief returns as warmth spreading through the soul.

A kindness offered returns as expansion.

A love given freely returns as a deepening of being.

"There is no punishment here," Guruji said. "Only resonance."

Pain inflicted his pain *felt*.

Love given is expansion *experienced.*

This is why guilt dissolves. There is no enemy to defend against—only truth to be embraced. Every action reveals itself not as sin or virtue, but as *unfinished understanding.*

Wisdom Through Empathy

By feeling the consequences of its actions from every side, the soul gathers wisdom—not as information, but as embodied compassion.

"The Bhagavad Gita hints at this," Guruji said, "when it teaches that action binds only when understanding is absent. When knowledge dawns, the same action liberates."

In the Upanishadic vision, this process is not punishment—it is *vidya*, true knowing.

In the Puranas, it is why souls return—not to suffer again, but to *complete seeing.*

In Tibetan teachings of the *Bardo*, the soul encounters its own mind—undressed of illusion.

In the Garbha Upanishad, remembrance arises between lives, only to be veiled again at birth.

In the Bible, the soul is said to be weighed—not by deeds alone, but by the heart's truth.

And the Sufis say the Beloved shows the lover his own face—until love matures into unity.

Across traditions, the message remains strikingly consistent:

Understanding liberates.

Awareness reshapes destiny.

What the Soul Learns Here

Guruji said gently:

- Consequences are felt to awaken compassion, not to induce shame
- Empathy is the soul's most powerful teacher
- Forgiveness arises naturally through understanding, not effort
- Awareness, once gained, alters the trajectory of future becoming

"This," he said, "is why the soul is allowed to feel everything it once caused. Not because it must suffer—but because it must *understand*."

After a long pause, Guruji asked quietly:

"Why must the soul feel consequences directly?"

"How does empathy expand awareness?"

"Why does forgiveness feel like liberation?"

"And most importantly—can awareness rewrite future karma?"

The hall remained silent.

Rohith asked, "Guruji, why does the soul need to experience the consequences of its actions, rather than simply comprehend them with the mind?"

Rohith's question lingered in the hall like a soft bell after it had been struck.

"Guruji," he asked, his voice steady but searching, "why must the soul *feel* the consequences of its actions? Why is understanding not enough?"

Guruji closed his eyes for a moment, as though listening to something older than the question. When he spoke, his voice was gentle, yet carried the weight of lived truth.

"Because," he said, "the soul is not made of thoughts. It is made of *experience*."

He leaned forward slightly. "Tell me, Rohith—can you understand fire by reading about heat? Or must your hand feel its warmth to truly know it?"

A ripple of quiet recognition passed through the hall.

"Intellectual understanding," Guruji continued, "belongs to the mind. Consequence belongs to consciousness. The mind learns through concepts; the soul awakens through resonance."

Knowledge vs. Transformation

"In the Bhagavad Gita," Guruji said, "Krishna does not merely *explain* dharma to Arjuna—He places Arjuna directly into the fire of his own becoming."

He recited softly: *There is nothing as purifying as direct realisation* (Gita 4.38).

na hi jnanena sadrisham pavitramiha vidyate |

tatsvayam yogasansiddhah kalenatmani vindati | |

Meaning: In this world, nothing is as purifying as true knowledge. One who has attained inner clarity through sustained yogic practice realises this knowledge directly within the heart, in the fullness of time.

Guruji paused and said, "Krishna does not speak of borrowed knowledge or second-hand wisdom. He speaks of a knowing that *arises from within*—a knowing earned through lived discipline, inner struggle, and direct experience."

"Krishna could have removed Arjuna from the battlefield," Guruji continued, "but then wisdom would have remained abstract. Instead, Arjuna is asked to stand, to tremble, to grieve, and to face his confusion without escape. Only then does sight replace fear. Truth that is not lived does not liberate—it merely decorates the intellect."

Guruji then said softly, "Knowledge indeed has the power to purify, elevate, and unite one with the Divine. But a crucial distinction must be understood—between information and transformation."

"There is one kind of knowledge acquired through scripture, discourse, and instruction. This knowledge is necessary, but it is incomplete. It is like memorising a cookbook without ever entering the kitchen. One may recite recipes flawlessly, yet still remain hungry."

"In the same way," Guruji explained, "one may speak eloquently about the soul, the Divine, maya, karma, jnana, and bhakti. But until this knowledge is *lived*, it does not dissolve ignorance—it only refines language."

"When a seeker practices sadhana in alignment with this knowledge," he said, "the mind is gradually purified. And in that purified silence, realisation dawns—not as belief, not as theory, but as recognition."

"Then," Guruji said, "knowledge no longer points toward truth. It *becomes* truth. And what is realised in the heart cannot be lost, argued with, or forgotten—because it has been *lived*."

The King Who Understood, But Did Not Feel

Guruji said, "Let me narrate a story - There was once a king who knew all scriptures. He spoke eloquently of compassion, charity, and justice. Yet one day, disguised as a beggar, he wandered his own kingdom and tasted hunger, rejection, and humiliation. That night, he wept—not from guilt, but from awakening. His knowledge had been accurate, but incomplete."

"Until he *felt* what others felt," Guruji said, "his wisdom had no roots."

Knowing by Becoming

"The Upanishads are very clear," Guruji continued. *'yatra tv asya sarvam ātmāivābhūt' — Where all this becomes the Self.*

"To know something truly," he explained, "you must *become* it. Feeling consequences is the soul's way of becoming what it once touched unconsciously."

"Without this becoming," he added, "karma remains stored as vasana—unfinished understanding. Feeling completes the circuit."

The River of Feeling: An Analogy

"Imagine," Guruji said, "a stone thrown into a river. The mind can calculate the ripples. The soul must *enter the water.*"

"When the soul feels consequences, it does not drown—it learns the shape of the waves it created. Only then does it know how to move without disturbing the water again."

Echoes

"In the Bible," Guruji said softly, "it is written: *'As ye sow, so shall ye reap.'* Reaping is not punishment—it is harvest. The fruit must be tasted to know what was planted."

"And the Sufis," he smiled, "say:

'Knowledge that does not melt you is not knowledge—it is a burden.'

The heart must be softened, not just informed."

Why Feeling Liberates

Guruji's voice deepened.

"Feeling consequences does three sacred things:

- It turns knowledge into compassion
- It dissolves judgment by revealing shared humanity
- It transforms memory into wisdom

If the soul only understood intellectually, it would repeat its patterns with better explanations but the same blindness."

He paused, letting the silence teach.

"Feeling is not cruelty," he said at last. "It is mercy. It is how consciousness teaches itself to love."

Guruji looked at Rohith with warmth.

"The soul feels consequences because awareness grows through empathy, not analysis. Understanding tells you *what* you did. Feeling reveals *who you became* because of it."

"And when that is seen fully," he said, almost in a whisper,

"there is nothing left to repeat."

The hall remained silent—not from confusion, but from recognition.

Sujitha's question lingered in the hall like a bell whose echo refuses to fade.

"Guruji," she asked softly, "how does experiencing another's pain or joy dissolve the illusion of separation?"

Guruji closed his eyes, as if listening—not to the question, but to where it was arising from. When he spoke, his voice carried the gentleness of something remembered rather than taught.

"Because," he said, "separation survives only as long as feeling remains confined."

He paused.

"The moment you *feel* another's pain as your own, the boundary collapses. Not philosophically. Existentially."

He leaned forward slightly.

“Thought can debate unity for lifetimes. Feeling ends the argument in a single breath.”

The Fire That Refuses to Stay in One Place

Guruji said, “In the Bhagavad Gita, Krishna does not teach unity as an idea to be memorised. He reveals it as a *vision* that must be lived.”

He recited softly (Bhagavad Gita 13.28):

samam sarveshu bhuteshu tishthantam parameshvaram |

vinashyatsv avinashyantam yah pashyati sa pashyati ||

Meaning:

They alone truly see who perceive the Supreme Self abiding equally in all beings—imperishable amidst the perishable.

Guruji paused, allowing the words to settle.

“This verse does not say *thinking* the same,” he explained. “It says *seeing* the same. And this seeing is not done with the eyes—it arises through empathy.”

“When Arjuna stands on the battlefield, he is not paralysed by doubt alone. He is overwhelmed by recognition. The faces before him are no longer 'others.' Their suffering has already entered his own heart."

"The grief he fears inflicting does not remain external. It echoes back into his own being. This is why his bow slips from his hand—not from weakness, but from awakened perception."

Guruji's voice softened.

"Empathy is not emotional excess. It is the moment when the illusion of separateness begins to fracture. When another's pain is felt as one's own, unity ceases to be a philosophy—it becomes a lived truth."

He said quietly, "Like fire, consciousness does not remain confined to one form. Once it touches another, it spreads. And once it spreads, separation can no longer pretend to exist."

Salt in Water

Guruji said, "Let me narrate a story, In the Chandogya Upanishad, a father asks his son to dissolve salt in water and return the next day. When asked where the salt is, the son cannot find it—but every sip tastes the same."

Guruji smiled.

""That,' the father says, 'is the Self.'"

"In the same way," Guruji continued, "when you feel another's sorrow, you do not *enter* their pain—you discover what was already shared."

"Separation is like believing the salt belongs to one corner of the glass."

Why Pain Teaches Faster Than Philosophy

Guruji's voice grew quieter.

"Pain dissolves boundaries because it bypasses identity. When you watch someone suffer, and your chest tightens without permission—that is not morality. That is memory."

Guruji said, "The Self is not known through intellect, but through immediate recognition."

"Empathy is recognition without words."

He paused, then added, "This is why the soul review you heard about earlier is transformative. The soul does not *understand* what it caused—it *feels* it. And in that feeling, the illusion of 'I' and 'you' quietly dies."

The Cross and the Beloved

Guruji said, "In the Bible, Christ does not redeem the world by preaching alone. He redeems it by entering its suffering."

'Whatever you did to the least of these, you did to me.'

Guruji said, "This is not a metaphor. It is ontology."

"When suffering is felt as shared, salvation is no longer an event—it is a realisation."

He then added softly, "The cross is not a punishment. It is radical empathy."

The Sufi's Wine

Guruji said, "A lover once asked a Sufi master, 'How will I know God?' The master replied, 'When your tears fall for a stranger as they do for yourself.'"

"In Sufism," Guruji said, "love is not an emotion—it is the collapse of distance."

"The wine of love is so intoxicating because it erases the cup."

Why Joy Is Equally Transformative

"And joy," Guruji added, "does the same work."

"When another's happiness fills you without envy, the ego loosens its grip. The heart recognises itself everywhere."

"Pain breaks the walls. Joy melts them."

Guruji looked at Sujitha.

"When you truly feel another's pain or joy, the mind cannot maintain the fiction of 'other.' The heart has already crossed the border."

He said:

- Separation is sustained by unshared feeling
- Empathy is unity remembered through sensation
- Pain teaches through contraction; joy through expansion
- When feeling is shared, identity dissolves naturally

"Unity," Guruji said, "is not achieved by thinking together—but by *feeling without edges*."

"Guruji," Akshaya asked softly, "why does forgiveness arise naturally from deep understanding, while guilt arises from incomplete awareness?"

Guruji did not answer immediately. He looked at the light falling on the floor, as though watching something ancient move through it.

“Because,” he said at last, “guilt belongs to the mind that still believes it stands apart. Forgiveness belongs to the heart that has remembered it was never separate.”

He leaned forward slightly.

“Let me tell you a story.”

The Child and the Broken Lamp

“A child once ran through his home at dusk, laughing, careless with joy. His foot struck a table, and a lamp shattered. Glass scattered. Darkness rushed in.

The child froze—not because of the broken lamp, but because of the fear of judgment. He stood there trembling, already punishing himself in imagination.

When the father entered, he did not ask *why*. He did not accuse. He simply lit another lamp and said, ‘Were you hurt?’

At that moment, the child wept—not from guilt, but from relief. The mistake dissolved, not because it was excused, but because it was understood.”

Guruji looked up.

"Guilt would have survived if the child believed the lamp mattered more than the relationship. Forgiveness arose because love revealed what truly mattered."

Why Guilt Persists

"Guilt," Guruji said, "is not repentance. It is resistance to seeing fully."

In incomplete awareness:

- The self is isolated
- Actions are labelled *mine*
- Consequences are feared, not felt
- The ego clings to the idea: *I should have been better*

"This is why guilt loops," Guruji explained. "It circles the wound without entering it."

In the **Great Life Review**, the soul does not *think* about what it did.

It *becomes* what it caused.

And the moment becoming happens, guilt loses its ground.

Understanding Transforms the Centre

Guruji said, "Ignorance is not moral failure—it is misidentification."

When awareness is incomplete, one says:

I hurt someone.

When awareness deepens, one realises:

I experienced myself as another.

This is why the *Bṛhadāraṇyaka Upanishad* teaches that liberation comes not when actions are erased, but when false identity dissolves.

"Forgiveness is not an act," Guruji said. "It is a consequence of expanded identity."

"In the Bhagavad Gita," Guruji said, "Krishna never tells Arjuna, 'Forgive yourself.' Instead, He widens Arjuna's vision until the doer collapses."

When Arjuna sees that the same consciousness moves through all beings, blame no longer has a single address.

"When the river knows it is the ocean," Guruji smiled, "it does not feel guilty for flooding a bank. It understands the tide."

The Sufis whisper a dangerous truth:

When the veil lifts, there is no sinner—only God learning Himself through form.

"Guilt survives where separation survives," Guruji said.

"Forgiveness arrives when the Beloved is seen in both the wound and the hand that struck."

"Even in the words of Jesus," Guruji continued, *'Father, forgive them, for they know not what they do.'*

"This is not moral superiority," he said. "It is perceptual clarity. Ignorance is named—not condemned."

Forgiveness here is not mercy from above—it is understanding from depth.

Why Forgiveness Is Liberation

Guruji said softly:

"Guilt binds the soul to the past by insisting, *I was wrong.*
Forgiveness releases the soul by realising that *I was unconscious.*

And unconsciousness is healed not by punishment—but by light."

He looked at Akshaya.

"When awareness completes itself, there is nothing left to forgive—only something understood."

Padma's question arrived gently, yet it carried the weight of lifetimes.

"Guruji," she asked, "once the soul has fully seen itself, how does this awareness influence the choices it will make in its next incarnation?"

Guruji closed his eyes for a moment, as though listening to something moving beneath words.

"When a soul has truly seen itself," he said softly, "choice is no longer reaction. It becomes response. And response is born of love, not compulsion."

From Blind Momentum to Conscious Direction

"Before awareness," Guruji explained, "the soul moves like a river in darkness—guided by terrain it cannot see. It flows where samskara pulls it, where unfinished understanding exerts gravity."

This is what the **Bhagavad Gita** calls *svabhava*—nature shaped by past impressions. Krishna tells Arjuna that beings act according to their nature, not because they are weak, but because momentum exists before insight.

"But," Guruji said, "when the soul has *seen*, momentum loses its blindness."

He paused.

"The river does not stop flowing. But now it knows where it is going."

The Story of the Archer

"Imagine," Guruji continued, "an archer who has spent lifetimes shooting arrows in fog. Sometimes they strike, sometimes they wound, sometimes they miss entirely. Each shot leaves a residue of consequence."

"One day, the fog lifts."

The archer sees the field clearly—for the first time. The targets are visible. The distance is known. The hands are steady.

"He does not forget how to shoot," Guruji said. "But now every arrow is intentional."

"This is how awareness reshapes incarnation."

Choice After the Great Seeing

"When the soul completes its deep seeing—through feeling every pain it caused, every love it offered—it does not choose blindly again."

The **Upanishads** describe this as movement from *avidya* (unseeing) to *vidya* (seeing). The soul no longer asks:

What do I want?

It asks:

- *What needs to be understood?*
- *Where can love mature further?*
- *What relationship will awaken what still sleeps in me?*

"Incarnation after awareness," Guruji said, "is not escape—it is refinement."

"In the Puranas," Guruji continued, "Vishnu descends again and again—not because He is bound, but because each descent serves a different aspect of dharma."

Rama incarnates to teach restraint and duty.

Krishna incarnates to teach love, play, and divine intimacy.

"These are not punishments," Guruji said. "They are *curricula* chosen by consciousness."

Likewise, a soul that has seen itself may choose:

- A quieter life to integrate wisdom
- A difficult life to dissolve subtle pride
- A loving life to deepen compassion
- A service-oriented life to balance past neglect

"Awareness does not seek comfort," Guruji smiled. "It seeks completion."

The Biblical Mirror

Guruji spoke gently, as though holding something fragile and luminous.

"In the Bible," he said, "it is written: *'To whom much is given, much will be required.'*" (Luke 12:48)

He paused, letting the words settle.

"This is not the language of judgment," he explained. "It is the language of alignment."

"When consciousness expands, life naturally asks more of it—not as punishment, but as expression. Just as a lamp that burns brighter illumines a wider space, a soul that has received deeper awareness cannot help but radiate it."

Guruji continued, "Responsibility does not arrive as a burden placed from outside. It rises from within as a capacity. Love, once known, cannot be unknown. Truth, once seen, cannot be unseen."

"A soul that has awakened may try to return to ignorance," he said softly, "but it will ache there—because it has outgrown that shelter."

"This pain is not guilt," Guruji said. "It is integrity calling the soul to live in harmony with what it already knows."

The Sufi Understanding

The Sufis say:

After awakening, the lover chooses suffering if it brings the Beloved closer.

Guruji nodded.

"Awakened souls may choose harder paths—not because they must, but because separation no longer frightens them."

"They know pain cannot harm the real."

How Karma Changes After Awareness

Guruji clarified:

"Before awareness, karma binds.

After awareness, karma instructs."

- Repetition becomes refinement
- Fate becomes dialogue
- Suffering becomes a teacher
- Choice becomes conscious participation

Guruji said, "This is why the wise act without bondage, even while acting fully."

The Quiet Truth

Guruji looked at Padma.

"When the soul has truly seen itself, it no longer incarnates to *become someone*."

"It incarnates to *express what it already knows*."

The hall felt vast, as though something unseen had taken a deeper breath.

"Awareness," Guruji said, "does not end birth. It ends unconscious birth."

And in that ending, a new kind of beginning waits.

CHAPTER VI

Stage Three

The Councils of the Soul

The soul does not ask for an easy life—it asks for the exact life that will wake it up."

– Shree Shambav.

Synopsis

This chapter explores Stage Three: The Councils of the Soul, revealing what unfolds after the soul has fully reviewed its past experiences. Rather than drifting in isolation, the soul enters a state of profound clarity where guidance arises through companionship, wisdom, and shared understanding. This realm is not a place of judgment or hierarchy, but a field of expanded awareness where truth is gently recognised, and readiness is lovingly assessed.

Through a symbolic story of a round table of knowing, the chapter illustrates how guiding intelligences—once encountered as teachers, adversaries, or loved ones—assist the soul in discerning what remains to be learned. Possible lives are revealed as living landscapes, each offering distinct opportunities for growth, healing, and service. Nothing is imposed; choice remains central.

Drawing parallels across spiritual traditions, the chapter emphasises that destiny is not enforced but co-created. Challenges are selected as instruments of evolution, and inner guidance during life is shown to be the echo of this pre-birth dialogue of remembrance.

"After the Great Life Review," Guruji said, "the soul is not left alone with its seeing. Understanding ripens best in companionship."

He paused.

"Guides. Masters. Loving intelligences.

Not external gods—but expanded consciousness aligned with your growth."

The soul, he explained, is gently ushered into a state of profound clarity. Not a *place* made of distance and direction, but a field of awareness where nothing needs to be defended and nothing is hidden. Light here does not dazzle—it *recognises.* Silence does not erase sound—it *contains* meaning.

"The soul senses presences," Guruji said, "not as strangers to be impressed, but as old friends remembered without names."

The Story of the Round Table

"Let me tell you a story."

Imagine arriving at a round table—not built of wood or stone, but of shared knowing. There is no 'head' of the table, because wisdom does not sit above—it surrounds.

Around you are beings you somehow recognise. Once came as your mother. One stood as your rival. One broke your heart. One held your hand when no one else did. One appeared only once in your life, briefly—but shifted its direction forever.

They do not speak with their mouths. Communication arrives whole—like understanding arriving before words.

No one asks, *Why did you fail?*

No one praises, *Look how well you did.*

Instead, there is a single, compassionate inquiry:

"What has been learned—and what still seeks experience?"

The wounds that still ache are touched—not to reopen them, but to ask what strength they are preparing. The talents you carry are acknowledged—not as medals, but as instruments.

Before you, lives appear—not fixed scripts, but living landscapes.

In one, you learn patience.

In another, you learn courage.

In another, you break an ancestral pattern carried for centuries.
In another, you learn love by losing it—and then learning to love without holding.

No voice commands.

No authority imposes.

"You choose," Guruji said softly.

"And the Council does not decide *for* you—they help you see *clearly*."

Not Judgment, but Maturity

"This," Guruji explained, "is not a court deciding punishment. It is a council assessing readiness."

In the **Upanishadic vision**, the soul is not dragged by fate but moves according to its ripeness. The **Brihadaranyaka** *Upanishad* speaks of the knower shaping their future movement according to what they have realised—not by decree, but by resonance.

In the **Bhagavad Gita**, Krishna echoes this when He says that beings are carried by their own nature (*svabhava*), yet liberated through awareness. The Council simply helps the soul recognise what its own nature is now ready to explore.

"Destiny," Guruji said, "is not imposed from above. It is *remembered from within*."

Echoes Across Traditions

Guruji continued, "sages speak of higher intelligences who guide souls between births—not as rulers, but as custodians of balance."

In the **Yoga Vasistha**, luminous beings guide the soul across worlds, reminding it of its freedom even while it chooses form.

In the **Bible**, angels appear not to dominate human will, but to *announce*, to *strengthen*, to *clarify*—'Fear not,' they say, again and again.

The **Sufis** speak of *friends of God*—invisible companions who whisper direction to the heart, not by instruction, but by attraction. Rumi writes of helpers who arrive the moment the soul becomes honest about its longing.

“Different languages,” Guruji said, “same compassion.”

The Last Reminder

Before the soul descends again, the Council offers no prophecy—only remembrance.

They remind the soul:

- of what it chose
- of what it may forget
- and of the quiet inner voice that will guide it again, even in the densest confusion

“That inner voice,” Guruji said, “is not imagination. It is the echo of this dialogue.”

Key Reflections

- Guidance exists before birth—not as control, but as collaboration

- Challenges are chosen for evolution, not assigned as punishment
- Destiny is co-created through awareness and readiness
- Inner guidance in life is the memory of this pre-birth clarity

Guruji let the silence return, then asked gently:

"Who do you think has been guiding you all along? Do you still believe your challenges are random? Have you noticed how dreams, intuitions, and sudden recognitions arrive—unannounced, yet precise?"

The hall remained still.

Dev asked, "Guruji, if guidance exists before birth, how does that reshape our understanding of destiny and the exercise of free will?"

Guruji listened quietly, then he spoke—not to answer immediately, but to open a horizon.

Destiny as a River, Free Will as the Oar

"Dev," Guruji said gently, "when guidance exists before birth, destiny is no longer a sentence—it becomes a **map drawn in love**."

He paused, then offered an image.

"Imagine a river that flows from the mountains to the sea. Its course is shaped long before you enter it—by gravity, terrain, and ancient movements of the earth. That river is destiny. But the boat you ride, the way you hold the oar, when you rest, when you row, when you turn toward the shore—this is free will."

"The river carries you. The oar reveals you."

The Gita: Freedom Within the Given Field

"In the Bhagavad Gita," Guruji continued, "Arjuna is not asked to choose whether the battlefield exists. It already does. But Krishna insists that Arjuna choose **how he stands within it**."

He quoted softly: Bhagavad Gita 3.8

niyatam kuru karma tvam karma jyayo hyakarmanah |

sharira-yatrapi cha te na prasiddhyed akarmanah | |

Guruji said, "You must, therefore, engage in your rightful action—not as compulsion, but as participation in life itself. For action is not merely preferable to inaction; it is the very current through which existence sustains itself. To withdraw from action is not freedom—it is stagnation. Even the body, this sacred instrument of experience, cannot be preserved through refusal to act."

"Perform your given duty, for action is better than inaction."

Guruji said, "Krishna is not advocating restless activity. He is revealing a **cosmic truth**:

Life moves through action.

To refuse action is not neutrality—it is resistance to the rhythm of being. Breath acts. Blood acts. Seasons act. The universe itself is a continuous offering of movement.

Even silence, when authentic, is an action of awareness.

Inaction born of fear, confusion, or avoidance does not liberate—it binds. It fragments the harmony between body, mind, and soul. When one abandons rightful action, the body decays, the mind dulls, and the soul contracts—not because action is punishment, but because **participation is nourishment**.

Guruji said, Krishna's teaching is subtle:

- Act, but without attachment
- Engage, but without ego
- Serve, but without claim

Guruji said, "True renunciation is not stepping away from life, but **moving within it without clinging**."

Action sustains the body.

Awareness sanctifies the action.

Together, they become the path to freedom.

"Destiny gives the field," Guruji explained. "Free will decides the **quality of consciousness** brought into that field."

And Krishna says again, with uncompromising honesty: Bhagavad Gita 18.60

swbhaava-jena kaunteya nibaddhah svena karmana |

kartum nechchhasi yan mohaat karishyasy avasho 'pi tat | |

Meaning: O Arjuna, bound by your own nature and shaped by your past actions, you will be compelled to perform the very action you resist out of confusion. Even against your conscious will, you will act—driven by your own inner disposition.

Guruji said softly,

"This is not Krishna denying freedom.

This is Krishna revealing **where freedom truly begins**."

He paused, allowing the weight of the verse to settle.

"Freedom does not start with choosing what happens outside you. It begins with seeing—clearly and honestly—what is already moving within you."

Krishna exposes a profound truth: beneath intention lies inclination; beneath choice lies conditioning; beneath resistance lies momentum older than thought. What we call *'I don't want this'* is often spoken by the surface mind, while a deeper current—*svabhava*, one's intrinsic nature—continues to flow.

This is why struggle persists. This is why patterns repeat. Not because the soul is weak, but because understanding is incomplete.

Guruji continued, "When action arises from unconscious nature, it feels like compulsion. When the same nature is seen with awareness, it becomes participation. Awareness does not erase movement—it transforms bondage into direction."

Guruji said:

You are not trapped by your nature.

You are invited to **know it**.

And in that knowing, what once pushed you blindly begins to serve you consciously.

Freedom, then, is not the absence of inner forces—it is intimacy with them.

The Weaver and the Thread

"Let me tell you a story," Guruji said.

"There was once a master weaver who prepared a loom for his apprentice before leaving the world. The loom was already strung—some threads coarse, some fine, some dark, some bright. When the apprentice returned, he cried, 'Why did you not leave me blank cloth?'

The master replied, 'Because you came to learn weaving, not avoidance.'

The apprentice could not change the threads already placed. But how he wove them—tight or loose, rushed or patient, resentful or reverent—changed the entire tapestry."

"The loom is destiny," Guruji said. "The weaving is free will."

Choice Within Law

"The Upanishads are clear," Guruji continued.

"The soul moves according to its knowledge."

yatha karma yatha srutam *(Brihadaranyaka Upanishad 4.4.5)*

Meaning: *As one acts, as one knows, so one becomes.*

Guruji said, "Pre-birth guidance does not cancel freedom—it **increases responsibility**. The more a soul knows, the more carefully it chooses. Ignorance feels random. Awareness feels intentional."

Chosen Burdens

Guruji said, "Great beings repeatedly accept difficult births."

Rama chooses exile.

Krishna chooses vulnerability.

Prahlada chooses persecution.

"Were these punishments?" Guruji asked softly.

"No. They were **alignments**."

"The soul does not choose ease—it chooses **growth**."

The Bible: Calling Before Arrival

"Even the Bible echoes this mystery," Guruji added.

'Before I formed you in the womb, I knew you.' (Jeremiah 1:5)

"This knowing is not surveillance," Guruji said. "It is **recognition**. The soul arrives already in conversation with purpose."

And yet:

'Choose this day whom you will serve.' (Joshua 24:15)

"Calling exists," Guruji smiled, "but choosing remains."

The Sufi Insight: The Beloved's Invitation

"The Sufis say," Guruji continued, 'The path was written before you walked it—but your footsteps make it real.'

Rumi writes: *'Why are you busy with this or that or good or bad; pay attention to how things blend.'*

"The Beloved invites," Guruji said. "The lover responds. Destiny is the invitation. Free will is the answer."

Guruji looked around the hall.

"When guidance exists before birth," he said slowly,

- Destiny is not coercion, but **context**
- Free will is not absolute control, but **conscious participation**
- Suffering is not random, but **meaningful terrain**

- Awakening is remembering why you agreed to walk here

"You are not puppets," Guruji said. "And you are not orphans."

"You are collaborators in your becoming."

He said softly:

"Destiny decides the questions. Free will decides whether you answer them with fear—or with love."

The hall remained silent—not because there was nothing left to say, but because something had been deeply understood.

John asked, "Guruji, why would a soul willingly choose hardship, limitation, or emotional pain as part of its journey?"

Guruji listened to John's question with a tenderness that suggested he had been waiting for it.

He did not answer immediately.

Instead, he looked at the flame of a small lamp nearby—steady, bright, unmoving—then spoke.

The Paradox of Chosen Pain

"John," Guruji said softly, "only a soul that is *already whole* can afford to choose difficulty."

The hall grew quiet.

"Pain chosen is not punishment. It is **curriculum**."

The Seed and the Stone

"Let me tell you a story," Guruji began.

A seed once lay in rich, dark soil. It was warm, nourished, untouched by struggle. Yet it did not grow. Nearby, another seed was pressed beneath a heavy stone. It cracked, strained, and suffered—but in breaking, it discovered its strength. Roots spread. A shoot rose. One day, it became a tree that offered shade even to the stone that once burdened it.

"The seed under the stone was not cursed," Guruji said. "It was *called*."

The Gita's Quiet Courage

"In the Bhagavad Gita," Guruji continued, "Krishna reveals this mystery when He says He enters the world by His own will."

'Though unborn and imperishable, I manifest Myself through My own power.' (Bhagavad Gita 4.6)

Guruji explained. "One descends because **relationship teaches what eternity alone cannot**. Limitation gives texture to wisdom. Resistance gives meaning to strength. Love discovered in separation is deeper than love assumed in unity."

Fire Learns Heat

"The Upanishads say," Guruji continued,

'The Self chooses its own path.' (Katha Upanishad 1.2.23)

"The soul is not dragged into suffering. It *leans* into it—like gold entering fire, not to be destroyed, but to be purified."

Pain reveals what comfort conceals.

In ease, the soul rests.

In hardship, it **awakens**.

The Story of King Bharata: The Love That Followed the Soul

Guruji began, "King Bharata was no ordinary ruler. He had conquered lands, governed with justice, and then—more difficult still—he conquered himself."

Bharata renounced his kingdom at the height of glory. He walked away from crowns and armies and chose the forest, carrying nothing but a begging bowl and the sacred Name in his breath. His days became quiet rivers of prayer. His nights, stars stitched into silence. He was free—or so it seemed.

One morning, near a riverbank, Bharata found a trembling fawn. Its mother had been swept away by the current. The small body shook with fear, eyes wide with helpless trust.

Something in Bharata broke open.

He lifted the fawn, fed it, and protected it. What began as compassion slowly became attachment. His meditation was shortened. His thoughts wandered. Instead of the Infinite, his mind circled the fragile life beside him.

Love had returned—disguised as care.

When death approached Bharata, his final breath did not rest in the Absolute. It rested on the deer.

And so, he was born again—as a deer.

Not a Fall, But a Fulfilment

"This," Guruji said gently, "is where many misunderstand the story."

Bharata's rebirth was not punishment. No divine judge condemned him. The universe did not strike him down.

He simply continued **where his attention had paused**.

As a deer, Bharata retained memory—not of pride or power, but of truth. He lived apart from the herd, grazing silently, eyes always alert. Even in an animal body, awareness burned bright. The soul had not fallen—it had followed its love to its conclusion.

"What bound him was not desire," Guruji said. "It was an incomplete presence."

The Return as Jada Bharata

In his next birth, Bharata returned as a human—Jada Bharata, the "silent one." He appeared dull, indifferent, broken by the world. People mocked him. Kings dismissed him. Yet within him lived vast clarity.

He had learned.

This time, he would not cling—not to power, not to affection, not even to spiritual pride. He walked untouched through praise and insult alike. When a king once threatened him, Bharata spoke—not with anger, but with cosmic calm—revealing knowledge that shattered illusion.

He had completed the lesson.

The Deeper Teaching

Guruji looked at John and said:

"The soul does not repeat because it is sinful.

It repeats because it is **unfinished**."

Unlived love returns.

Unseen truth revisits.

Uncompleted awareness asks again—gently, patiently.

Bharata did not return to suffer.

He returned to **see clearly what he once saw partially**.

"The universe," Guruji whispered, "is not punitive. It is pedagogical."

The Mirror for All Souls

"When something loops in your life," Guruji said, "a relationship, a pain, a longing—do not ask, 'What is wrong with me?'

Ask instead, 'What am I being invited to see more consciously?'"

For the soul, love never ends.

It only deepens—until it is finally free.

And that, Guruji said, "is grace wearing the face of repetition."

Guruji paused, letting the weight of many scriptures settle into the room.

"**Even in the Bible, the pattern is clear,**" he said softly—not as doctrine, but as recognition.

Joseph is betrayed by his own brothers and thrown into a pit.

Job is stripped of wealth, family, health—until even language fails him.

Christ accepts the cross, not in defeat, but in conscious surrender.

"These are not stories of divine cruelty," Guruji said. "They are maps of inner expansion."

Joseph's suffering enlarges him. The pit becomes a womb. Betrayal trains his vision until he can hold power without revenge. When he finally stands before his brothers, he does not punish—he forgives. Suffering has increased his **capacity for mercy**.

Job's trials do not teach him obedience; they strip him of explanations. His pain dismantles borrowed beliefs until he meets divine not through theology, but through presence: *'I had heard of You by the hearing of the ear, but now my eye sees You.'* Suffering here deepens **perception**.

And Christ—fully aware—does not flee pain. He enters it freely, transforming the cross from an instrument of death into a bridge of compassion. As Hebrews says: *"Though He was a Son, yet He learned obedience through suffering."* Not obedience to punishment—but obedience to love.

"Suffering," Guruji said, "is not inflicted to break the soul. It is enduring to **stretch it**—so it can carry truth without collapsing, power without corruption, and love without fear."

"This," he said quietly, "is not cruelty. It is capacity-building."

The Sufi's Burning

The Sufis speak of this with fierce beauty.

Rumi writes:

'Why are you so busy with this or that, good or bad; pay attention to how things blend.'

"The moth does not fly into the flame because it hates itself," Guruji smiled. "It flies because it loves the light more than safety."

Pain chosen by the soul is **love choosing truth over comfort**.

Why the Soul Chooses Hardship

Guruji turned back to John.

"The soul chooses limitation for four reasons," he said gently:

- **To develop compassion** — empathy cannot be imagined; it must be lived
- **To dissolve ego** — comfort rarely questions identity
- **To complete unfinished understanding** — what was avoided returns as the teacher
- **To remember itself more deeply** — forgetting sharpens recognition

"A soul that has never been broken cannot know tenderness," Guruji added.

"A soul that has never been lost cannot guide others home."

"Pain," Guruji said, "is not chosen because it is desirable—but because it is *effective.*"

Not all pain is sacred.

But pain entered **consciously**, met with awareness, and became alchemy.

"'The soul does not ask, 'Will this hurt?'

It asks, 'Will this awaken?'"

He paused, then asked John quietly:

"When you look back at your own hardest moments—

were they merely wounds…

or were they doors?"

Nita asked, "Guruji, could our dreams, intuitions, and sudden insights be whispers of agreements made with the Council before birth?"

Guruji closed his eyes for a moment, as if listening inwardly. When he spoke, his voice was gentle, almost intimate.

"Nita," he said, "before a soul is clothed in flesh, it is clothed in *knowing*. But birth is a veil, not an erasure. What was once clear becomes faint—like a melody heard through water. Dreams, intuition, sudden insight… these are ripples from that deeper remembering."

He continued, "In the **Upanishads**, it is said that the Self moves in three states—waking, dreaming, and deep sleep—and that in dreams, the soul roams closer to its source. When the mind loosens its grip, the ancient memory breathes again. That is why guidance often arrives not as commands, but as symbols—a door, a river, a forgotten face."

Guruji's smile lingered, as though the story had already begun long before the words.

"Imagine," he said, "a traveller standing at the edge of a vast forest just before dawn. The trees rise like ancient questions, their roots tangled with shadows, their canopies thick enough to hide the sky. The path beyond the first step is invisible. Once he enters, there will be no maps, no voices, no certainty—only choice."

"Before he steps in, a small circle gathers around him. They are not strangers. Some have walked with him before, some have shaped him quietly, some have opposed him so fiercely that he grew because of them. They do not speak with urgency. They sit together, calm, attentive, loving."

"They study the forest—not to control it, but to understand its rhythms. They say, *There will be moments when you feel lost. In those moments, look for signs.* One says, *When you see the great banyan tree—wide, rooted, sheltering—pause and turn left. That is the way of patience.* Another says, *When night falls, and fear grows quiet, listen. If you hear a river flowing in the dark, you are close to home, even if you cannot yet see it.*"

"The traveller listens. He understands. He agrees. Not because he is forced, but because something in him recognises the truth of their words. Then he steps forward."

"As soon as he enters the forest, the world changes. The light dims. The companions are gone. The agreements fade into feeling rather than memory. The traveller walks, stumbles, learns. He mistakes shadows for threats and silence for abandonment. Many times, he believes he has chosen the wrong path."

"But one day, exhausted and unsure, he comes upon a massive banyan tree. Its branches hang low, offering rest. Something in him slows. He does not know why—but he turns left."

"Another night, when despair presses heavily on his chest, he hears water moving somewhere beyond the dark. He cannot see it, yet his heart softens. He feels nearer to home than he has in years."

Guruji's voice softened.

"The traveller does not remember the meeting at the forest's edge. But the forest remembers him. The signs remember him."

"Life," Guruji said, "is the forest. Birth is the forgetting. And intuition, dreams, sudden recognition—these are the signs left behind by a wiser version of yourself."

"They are not commands. They are reminders. And when you follow them, you are not obeying something outside—you are keeping a promise you once made to your own soul."

"Dreams are banyan trees," Guruji said. "Intuition is the sound of the river."

Guruji said, "The sages or enlightened souls receive sudden revelations not through effort, but remembrance. In the **Bible**, Joseph is guided through dreams, not arguments. In **Sufi** lore, Rumi says, *Why are you busy with the letters when the message has already reached your heart?*"

"These moments feel sudden because they bypass thought. They arrive whole—like recognition, not discovery. You do not reason them out; you *remember* them."

Guruji said softly, "The Council does not speak in sentences. It whispers in symbols, nudges, unrest, and clarity. When you follow these inner movements, life flows with an uncanny rightness. When you resist them, there is friction."

"Dreams, intuition, insight—these are not interruptions to your life. They are **footnotes written by your deeper self**, reminding you of agreements made in love, before you ever forgot who you were."

Lalitha asked, "Guruji, what practices in daily life help us reconnect and hear this inner guidance with clarity once more?"

Guruji closed his eyes for a moment, as though listening to something older than the hall, older than language itself.

"Lalitha," he said gently, "guidance is never absent. What changes is our capacity to hear."

He paused, then began a story.

The Dust on the Mirror

Guruji's voice softened, as though he were no longer teaching but remembering aloud.

"Imagine," he said, "a vast palace with a thousand rooms—corridors opening into corridors, chambers once filled with music, prayer, laughter, and silence. At the very centre of this palace hangs a mirror unlike any other. It is not made merely of glass. It is alive with clarity. When it is clean, it reflects not the walls around it, but the open sky itself—clouds passing, stars turning, dawn arriving without effort.

This mirror was never meant to be admired. It was meant to guide. Anyone who stood before it could see where they were, where they had wandered, and where the light was coming from.

But over time, the palace is abandoned.

No storm destroys it. No thief breaks in. Dust simply begins to settle—slowly, patiently. One grain from an unspoken fear. Another from a compromise made in exhaustion. Another from a desire chased without listening. The dust does not arrive as sin or failure; it arrives as forgetfulness.

The mirror does not crack. It does not protest. It does not lose its nature. It only grows dim.

Those who enter the palace later assume the mirror is old, useless, or broken. Some try to replace it with lamps. Others decorate the walls, hoping brightness will come from outside. But the mirror waits—silent, unchanged, faithful to what it has always been.

"Our lives," Guruji continued, "are exactly like this palace."

"The rooms are our many roles—child, parent, seeker, worker, lover, mourner. Some rooms we visit daily. Others we lock and avoid. But at the centre of it all hangs the mirror—the inner guide."

"This is the *antaratman* the Upaniṣads speak of: smaller than the smallest, greater than the greatest. This is the *Paramatma* revealed in the Gita, dwelling equally in all beings. This is the 'still small voice' Elijah hears after the storm and the fire. This is the *sirr* the Sufis whisper about—the secret of secrets, where God speaks without sound."

"It does not command. It does not argue. It does not threaten. It reflects."

Guruji paused, letting the image settle.

"When we feel lost," he said gently, "it is not because guidance has disappeared. It is because the mirror has been covered—by noise, by fear, by relentless doing, by forgetting how to be still."

He smiled, almost tenderly.

"That is why the practices are so simple—and so misunderstood. They are not about creating wisdom. They are not about becoming worthy of guidance. They are about wiping the dust."

"Each moment of honesty is a cloth. Each act of compassion is a clearing breath. Each silence entered willingly is a hand restoring the mirror's face."

"And when even a small patch becomes clear," Guruji said, his eyes shining, "the sky rushes back in—effortlessly, completely, as if it had been waiting all along."

Acting Without Noise

Guruji's voice was steady, but there was a quiet joy in it, as if he were revealing a secret hidden in plain sight.

"In the *Bhagavad Gita* (2.50)," he said, "Krishna does not ask Arjuna to flee the world, nor to paralyse himself in the name of spirituality. He asks him to *refine the way he acts.*"

He recited slowly:

buddhi-yukto jahatiha ubhe sukrita-dushkrite |

tasmad yogaya yujyasva yogah karmasu kaushalam | |

Meaning: "Endowed with clarity of intelligence, one releases attachment to both virtue and vice. Therefore, commit yourself to Yoga—*for Yoga is skill in action*."

"Notice," Guruji explained, "Krishna does not define Yoga as withdrawal, ritual, or belief. He defines it as *kaushalam*—skill, intelligence, precision in how action arises from consciousness."

Guruji said, "To act without craving for reward, and without fear of loss—this is purification. Such action leaves no residue. It neither inflates the ego through 'good deeds' nor burdens the heart with regret over 'bad outcomes.' It passes through the soul like wind through an open window."

He paused, then offered an image.

"A restless lake," Guruji said, "cannot reflect the moon, no matter how bright the moon is. The moon does not withhold its light—the water simply cannot hold it. But when the waters grow still, reflection is effortless. Nothing new is added. Nothing is forced."

"In the same way," he continued, "when action is purified of grasping and anxiety, the mind naturally becomes quiet. And in that quiet, guidance is no longer drowned out. The inner voice was always speaking—but only silence could hear it."

"Yoga," Guruji smiled, "is not escaping action. It is acting so cleanly that awareness shines through it."

Learning to Sit with the Flame

Guruji spoke gently, as if careful not to disturb something subtle already stirring in the hall.

"The *Upaniṣads* do not rush the seeker toward conclusions," he said. "They offer a rhythm of ripening: **sravana, manana, nididhyāsana**—first listening, then reflecting, and finally deep, steady contemplation."

"Sravana is not mere hearing," Guruji explained. "It is allowing truth to enter without argument. *Manana* is turning that truth within, like holding a flame in the palm—not to extinguish it, but to feel its warmth. And *nididhyāsana* is learning to sit with that flame long enough that it reshapes you."

He paused.

"Most suffering comes from our impatience with not-knowing. We want answers quickly, so we silence the question before it has done its sacred work. But wisdom is not born from hurried certainty—it is born from intimacy with the unresolved."

Guruji smiled softly.

"Many people pray only to speak—to ask, to plead, to explain themselves to the divine. The wise pray to listen. They sit quietly, not demanding replies, trusting that truth reveals itself when the mind stops interrupting."

"Learning to sit with the flame," he said, "is learning to trust that light does not need to be chased. It needs space."

Entering the Inner Room

Guruji's voice softened, as though inviting the listeners inward.

Matthew, Chapter 6, Verse 6

"Jesus said, *'When you pray, go into your inner room and shut the door.'*"

He paused. "This is not architecture—it is **attention**."

"The *inner room* is the place where the world's demands fall silent. It is not reached by distance, but by withdrawal—from noise, from comparison, from the endless rehearsal of who we think we must be. To *shut the door* is to close the mind's habit of commentary, self-judgment, and performance."

He continued, "Most people try to hear guidance while standing in a marketplace of thoughts. But truth does not compete. It waits."

"When the heart is no longer busy defending itself, it becomes a sanctuary again. In that quiet, something ancient stirs—the same stillness Elijah encountered, the same presence the Upaniṣads call the *antaratman*."

Guruji smiled gently.

"Guidance does not shout, threaten, or persuade. It whispers. And only those who dare to become quiet enough discover that the whisper has been there all along—patient, intimate, and faithful."

Polishing the Heart

Guruji spoke slowly, as if each word were itself an act of remembrance.

"The Sufis say the heart is a mirror," he said, "but not a broken one—only a forgotten one. Its dullness is not a flaw; it is rust gathered from living too long without looking inward."

"*Dhikr*—the remembrance of the Beloved—is not repetition meant to inform God of our devotion. God is not forgetful. **We are.** Each name, each breath of remembrance, is a gentle stroke of the cloth against the mirror of the heart."

He paused, letting the image settle.

"When the heart remembers, it softens. When it softens, it reflects. And when it reflects clearly, guidance appears without effort—like a face revealed in still water."

Guruji smiled.

"Love is the fastest solvent because it does not argue with the rust. It does not condemn the forgetting. It simply stays present long enough for the heart to remember its own brightness."

"Truth does not arrive by force," he said quietly. "It shines the moment the mirror is clean enough to receive it."

The Simple Truth

Finally, Guruji looked at Lalitha and said,

"Practices that restore guidance are simple, but not easy:

- Silence that is honest, not forced
- Action done as offering, not ambition
- Attention to dreams and intuition without obsession
- Compassion, because cruelty makes the heart noisy
- And above all—sincerity"

He smiled.

"When the life you live aligns even slightly with the life you agreed to live, the guidance grows louder. Not as words—but as peace. And peace," he said softly, "is the surest sign you are listening again."

After a long, luminous pause, Guruji rose from his asana. He did not announce the end; he *embodied* it. His departure was as silent as his presence had been full. Without a final word, he left the Buddha Hall, as one leaves a lamp burning in the heart rather than in the room.

One by one, the devotees stood and drifted away.

The hall emptied of human form, yet it did not feel vacant. The air still carried warmth—as if the teachings had soaked into the walls, the floor, the very silence itself. Outside, the night had fully arrived. The sky stretched wide and clear, stars blinking in and out as thin clouds played their quiet game of hide and seek. The wind moved softly through the courtyards, brushing leaves together in a whispering language older than speech. Frogs croaked their nocturnal hymns, insects hummed in patient rhythm, and somewhere in the distance, night birds called out—long, echoing notes that sounded like questions flung gently into the dark.

Even in stillness, the world was speaking.

Drawn by the hunger of a simpler kind, the devotees made their way toward the food centre. The path felt lighter now, as if the weight of the day had been rearranged rather than removed.

At the Annapoorneswari food centre, warmth returned in another form. The air was thick with the aroma of spices, steaming idlis, crisp dosas, and the earthy comfort of South Indian dishes prepared with quiet devotion. Plates were filled, hands folded briefly in gratitude, and conversations softened into smiles as nourishment reached the body.

After the meal, something unspoken pulled many of them toward the fireplace.

Vidyarthi, Aastha, Akshaya, Kiran, Padma, Vasudeva, and Abhirami settled around the flames. Firelight danced across their faces, throwing flickering shadows that made each expression look deeper, more alive. The crackle of burning wood became a companion to their voices. They spoke of the day—of insights that had unsettled them, questions that refused to rest, moments when Guruji's words had landed like arrows or like balm. Laughter rose too, easy and unforced, as small human missteps were remembered and gently forgiven.

Soon, others arrived, drawn by the glow and the quiet joy it held. Bhavya, Aarna, Dev, Kiran, Sam, Alice, Sofia, and John joined the circle, their footsteps still carrying the calm of an evening walk. Their presence widened the circle, as if the fire itself had room for more listening. Then came Nita, Lalitha, Rohith, and Sujitha, adding new tones to the conversation—soft reflections, sudden insights, nods of recognition.

Moments later, Akshatha, Apeksha, Abhilasha, Akanksh, Roopa, and others appeared, their faces still luminous with contemplation. Behind them came Kieron, Astyn, Espen, Greta, and Divyani, each carrying that familiar, shared silence of seekers who know they are walking the same inner terrain, even when their questions differ.

The fire burned steadily now.

Akshatha's voice rose—not loud, but clear—cutting gently through the murmurs.

"Time for Apeksha's story…"

The circle shifted. Bodies leaned forward. Eyes turned. The flames seemed to listen too.

Apeksha inhaled deeply, as if drawing courage from the fire, from the night, from the unseen thread that bound them all. And she began.

The Lamp That Remembered

“Once,” Apeksha began, “there was a small oil lamp kept in a mountain monastery. It was not the largest lamp, nor the brightest. It stood near a stone pillar, often overlooked. Yet every evening, without fail, a monk would light it before night prayers.”

“One winter, a violent storm swept through the valley. Winds howled, roofs shook, and many lamps inside the monastery went out. When morning came, the monks found something strange—the small lamp near the pillar was still burning.”

“They asked the old caretaker how this was possible.”

“He smiled and said, ‘That lamp was placed where the wind could not reach it. It did not fight the storm. It stood where remembrance was stronger than fear.’”

Apeksha paused, her voice softening.

“But the story does not end there.”

“One day, the monk who used to light the lamp did not return. Days passed. The oil ran low. The flame weakened. At last, it went out.”

“The lamp was not broken. The wick was not damaged. Only the remembering hand was absent.”

She looked around the circle.

"Years later, a traveller came seeking shelter. In the darkness, he stumbled, struck the pillar, and found the cold metal of the lamp. Something stirred in him—an unexplainable familiarity. He filled it with oil, struck a flame, and lit it."

"The lamp burned again—not because it was new, but because it remembered what it was made for."

Apeksha let the silence deepen before continuing.

"The soul is like that lamp," she said. "Before birth, it is placed carefully—by wisdom, by love, by councils we no longer remember. Then we enter the storm of life. Wind comes as desire. Cold comes as fear. Forgetting comes as identity."

"When we suffer, it is not because the lamp is weak. It is because the hand that remembers has not yet returned."

She glanced toward the fire.

"Dreams, sudden intuitions, moments when something inside us says *'This way'*—these are not random. They are the traveller's hand. They are echoes of agreements made before the storm."

The fire crackled sharply, as if punctuating her words.

"Some of us feel restless. Some feel called. Some feel tired without knowing why. It is not because life is wrong."

"It is because the lamp is asking to be lit again."

Apeksha smiled gently.

"And when it is—

the storm does not stop,

but the flame no longer fears it."

No one spoke for a long time.

The fire burned lower. The night deepened. And somewhere between breath and silence, each listener felt something familiar—

not learned,

not new,

but remembered.

Later—much later—one by one, the devotees rose. There was no rush. Each movement felt deliberate, tender. The night held them as a mother who knows her children will return. As they walked toward their chambers, the lessons of the day did not fade; they followed quietly, settling into thought, breath, and dream.

And thus, the night became more than darkness.

It became a sanctuary—a bridge between what had been heard and what was yet to be lived. A reminder that teaching does not end with words, that guidance continues in firelight, shared silence, and starlit skies. Even now, under the vast patience of the heavens, life was still instructing—softly, steadily, endlessly.

EPILOGUE

The Door That Was Never Closed

"Even when the world rages around you, gratitude keeps your inner light steady. The smallest flame, tended with awareness, can guide you through the darkest night."

– *Shree Shambav.*

This book began before the first page and ends without truly ending.

What you have read is not a map of distant heavens or an argument about unseen worlds. It is a remembering—gentle, unsettling, intimate—of something the soul already knows but the mind has forgotten. *Before we were born*, there was intention. Before breath, there was listening. Before destiny, there was dialogue.

In **Part One**, we traced the outlines of the Eternal Architect—not as an external authority, but as intelligence woven into existence itself. We explored the soul not as a fragment seeking repair, but as consciousness choosing experience. We followed prana as the bridge between worlds, karma as mathematics rather than moral judgment, and memory as movement rather than burden.

In **The Sacred Preparation**, the veil lifted further. We saw that incarnation is not an accident, nor a punishment, nor a blind fall into matter. It is a sacred consent. The Call of Universal Consciousness revealed longing as the echo of fullness. The Great Life Review showed that understanding is born not from judgment, but from feeling. And the Councils of the Soul reminded us that destiny is not imposed—it is co-authored with wisdom, compassion, and love.

Yet even here, something remains unfinished.

That is not a flaw in the teaching. It is its nature.

Because this book was never meant to give you final answers. It was meant to return you to the right questions—the ones that stir quietly beneath ambition, fear, success, and sorrow. The questions that arise when you pause long enough to listen.

You may close this book, but the process it points to does not close. It continues in your choices, your restlessness, your moments of sudden clarity, your inexplicable attractions and resistances. It continues each time life asks more of you than comfort, and each time love asks more of you than certainty.

If there is one truth this part leaves you with, let it be this:

You are not here by accident.

You are not learning blindly.

And you are not alone in your becoming.

The remaining stages—the deeper mechanics of choice, the mystery of forgetting and remembering, the final truth that dissolves even the idea of stages—will be explored in **Part Two**. Not as continuation, but as deepening. Not as revelation from above, but as recognition from within.

Until then, walk gently.

Notice what moves you before thought.

Listen to what repeats.

Trust the quiet intelligence shaping your life from behind the veil.

The soul remembers the way—even when the mind does not.

And the door you think you are searching for

was never locked.

Life Coach and Philanthropist

Shree Shambav is the visionary founder of the Shree Shambav Ayur Rakshita Foundation (www.shambav-ayurrakshita.org). He founded this institution with a lofty goal: to recognise human identity across gender, ethnicity, and nationality. Through this organisation, he wants to assist all communities in realising their full potential and the intrinsic beauty of life.

Shree Shambav, a Life Coach, is dedicated to supporting people on their journeys of self-discovery and empowerment. He assists people in discovering who they are, determining what inspires and drives them, and overcoming limiting ideas. His approach clarifies what one wants in life, assisting people through goal-setting and a step-by-step process for achieving them. He empowers people to make deliberate and responsible decisions, allowing them to identify their blind spots and evolve as individuals via the use of numerous strategies and tools.

The foundation's bold, uncompromising, and compassionate ventures are always aimed at initiating the "Inner Transformation" process. They focus on spiritual growth, personal growth, and self-healing while emphasising that true progress lies in "Inclusive Growth and Co-existence." This philosophy drives all their initiatives, encouraging a holistic approach to development and well-being.

Under Shree Shambav's leadership, the foundation has launched several impactful movements:

Shree Shambav Green Movement: This mission is to create a healthy, green, and clean earth through responsible water conservation and greening initiatives. The movement strives to make the world a green paradise by encouraging sustainable living and environmental responsibility.

Shree Shambav Vidya Vedhika (Vizhuthugal): This project aims to help students and children by offering training, books, stationery, and uniforms. It aims to provide the next generation with the tools and resources they need to excel both academically and personally.

Shree Shambav and his foundation exemplify the spirit of compassion, transformation, and inclusive growth via their work, which has a profound impact on individuals and communities around the world. His work exemplifies the power of acknowledging and nourishing the human spirit, creating a world in which everyone can reach their full potential and appreciate the beauty of life.

TESTIMONIALS

Journey of Soul - Karma - “We die in our twenties and are buried at eighty.” Remember that nothing can stop someone who refuses to be stopped. “Most people do not fail; they simply give up.” Shree Shambav deserves full credit. It allowed me to sit and consider what I might miss out on in life. The author has delved into every aspect of our daily lives. How can a seemingly insignificant change in these seemingly insignificant details bring us such joy? The Soul of Journey teaches you the “art of living” as well as the “art of dying.”

Twenty + One Series - The rich cultural heritage offered a host in twenty + one short stories with incredible imagination, morals and values prevalent at a given time, influencing how people respond to a crisis or any situation. The author has recreated images with universal values and morals. The plentiful of fascinating from faraway lands would leave the modern play and story writers a cringe. The book supports trust and immeasurable values instilling hope for the new generations.

Death - "Shree Shambav's 'Death - Light of Life and the Shadow of Death' is an extraordinary masterpiece that delves deep into the profound questions surrounding our existence and mortality. The book's opening statement, 'Nothing ever truly dies; it simply ceases to exist in one form before resuming it in another,' sets the stage for a thought-provoking exploration of death's multifaceted nature. Shambav's remarkable ability to navigate the philosophical complexities of death and our universal fear of it is both enlightening and comforting. This book is a testament to the power of understanding and acceptance."

Whispers of Eternity - "Reading 'Whispers of Eternity' by Shree Shambav was a transformative experience that left me captivated from beginning to end. Each section of this exquisite collection delves into the myriad facets of existence, offering poignant reflections on life, death, and everything in between. Shree Shambav's verses are a testament to the beauty of language and the power of expression, inviting readers to embark on a journey of self-discovery and spiritual awakening. Whether celebrating life's simple joys or grappling with the complexities of human emotion, this book is a timeless companion that speaks to the heart and soul of every reader."

Life Changing Journey Series - "Life Changing Journey Series II Inspirational Quotes" is a remarkable collection that illuminates the path to self-discovery and personal growth. With its inspiring quotes and insightful reflections, this book serves as a beacon of light in a world often shrouded in darkness. Each quote offers wisdom, guidance, and encouragement, reminding readers of their inner strength and resilience. A must-read for anyone seeking inspiration and enlightenment.

Learn To Love Yourself – "A Heartfelt Guide to Authentic Self-Love." "Learn to Love Yourself" invites readers on a transformative journey to embrace their true essence in a world often focused on external validation. Through ten insightful chapters, it gently reveals principles of genuine self-love, guiding readers to deepen their connection with themselves. Beyond surface positivity, it encourages the cultivation of resilient self-acceptance, from embracing one's unique qualities to setting empowering boundaries. With inspiring stories and practical wisdom, this book is a trusted companion on the path to inner peace, fulfilment, and joy, helping readers build lives that reflect their authentic selves.

The Power of Letting Go – This book has been a gift to my spiritual journey. Shree Shambav's insights into attachment, personal growth cycles, and forgiveness are enlightening. The concept of seven-year cycles resonated with me, helping me understand the natural phases of life. I feel more empowered to let go of what no longer serves me and step into a life of freedom and fulfilment. A truly beautiful read!

A Journey of Lasting Peace – "A Journey of Lasting Peace" feels like a trusted friend guiding you through the maze of self-discovery. The 18 transformative principles are both practical and deeply resonant, addressing everything from gratitude practices to the art of letting go. Each chapter is infused with warmth and wisdom, making it easy to apply the concepts to my life. I particularly appreciated the emphasis on physical health's connection to mental well-being; it served as a wake-up call for me to prioritise my health. This book is an invaluable resource for anyone serious about personal growth!

Astrology Unveiled Series – "Profound, Logical, and Inspiring". What stands out in Astrology Unveiled is the author's dedication to making Vedic astrology logical and approachable. Each concept flows naturally into the next, backed by examples and exercises. The insights into karma and life cycles add a philosophical depth rarely seen in astrology books. Perfect for anyone seeking spiritual growth alongside astrological knowledge!

The Entitlement Trap - "Thought-Provoking and Challenging" The book challenges readers to confront their own sense of entitlement, and that's not easy—but it's essential. The Entitlement Trap doesn't offer a one-size-fits-all approach. Instead, it's a thoughtful, layered examination of how entitlement can limit our growth. The chapter on "Defining Your Own Hill" was particularly impactful, as it pushed me to reconsider which challenges are truly worth pursuing. A thought-provoking read for those willing to do the inner work to create a life they can be proud of.

Whispers of a Dying Soul – "A Soul-Stirring Reflection on Life's Unspoken Truths" - *Whispers of a Dying Soul: Unspoken Regrets and Unlived Dreams"* is a deeply moving exploration of the unexpressed emotions and unfulfilled aspirations that shape our lives in ways we often don't realise. This book invites readers to confront the powerful, often hidden impact of regret while guiding them through a journey of introspection and healing. Each page opens a space to reflect on the choices that define us—from moments of unspoken love to neglected passions—offering a gentle reminder to live authentically and courageously.

Whispers of the Soul: A Journey Through Haiku - is a mesmerising collection that speaks directly to the heart. Each haiku is a delicate brushstroke capturing life's fleeting beauty and timeless wisdom, inviting readers into moments of deep reflection and peace. This book is a balm for the soul, guiding us to find meaning in stillness and connection in simplicity. The themes of nature, love, and mindfulness echo universal truths, resonating with quiet, powerful grace. It's a book to be savoured slowly, cherished deeply, and returned to often. Truly, a gift for anyone seeking calm and clarity in life's chaos.

Whispers of Silence - Unlocking Inner Power through Stillness by Shree Shambav is a rare gem that beckons readers to pause, reflect, and reconnect with their inner selves. In a world that never stops talking, this book offers a profound exploration of silence—not as a void but as a rich and transformative space.

From the first page, Shree Shambav's writing resonates deeply, blending scientific insights with spiritual wisdom in a way that feels both universal and deeply personal. The author's ability to bridge the tangible and the transcendent makes this book an invaluable guide for anyone navigating the chaos of modern life.

The Power of Words: Transforming Speech, Transforming Lives - "The Power of Words is a profound and enlightening guide that has transformed the way I approach communication. Shree Shambav masterfully uncovers the hidden influence of our words on relationships, self-perception, and overall well-being. This book doesn't just teach you how to speak; it inspires mindful communication that fosters connection and trust. The insights on replacing negative patterns like gossip and judgment with kindness and authenticity are truly life-changing. The practical strategies and engaging narratives make it an invaluable resource for personal and professional growth. A must-read for anyone striving to communicate with intention, clarity, and compassion. Highly recommended!"

The Art of Intentional Living: Minimalism for a Life of Purpose - "The Art of Intentional Living is a refreshing guide to finding clarity in a cluttered world. With practical wisdom and profound insights, it inspires you to simplify, prioritise, and live with purpose. A must-read for anyone seeking balance and fulfilment."

Awakening the Infinite: The Power of Consciousness in Transforming Life - "Awakening the Infinite is a transformative guide that expands the mind and nourishes the soul. With profound insights and practical wisdom, this book beautifully explores the power of consciousness, helping readers connect with their true purpose and inner potential. It is a journey of self-discovery, healing, and spiritual awakening, offering clarity and inspiration at every turn. A must-read for anyone looking to live with greater awareness, meaning, and authenticity."

Beyond the Veil: A Journey Through Life After Death:

"This book touched me in ways few others have—it's not just about death, but about life, meaning, and the vast unknown that connects them. Beyond the Veil offers a graceful blend of science and spirit, inviting us to explore the mystery with awe rather than fear. The stories, insights, and reflections linger in your heart long after the final page. A truly transformative read that brings light on the shadows of mortality. It reminded me that in embracing death, we truly learn how to live."

Bonds Beyond Blood:

"A profoundly moving story that reminds us, family is not defined by blood, but by love, sacrifice, and the courage to heal. Every chapter touched my soul with its emotional truth and timeless wisdom. Through joy, grief, and redemption, this book captures the raw beauty of human connection. I saw reflections of my own family in its pages—both the pain and the hope. A powerful, unforgettable read that lingers long after the final word."

A Journey into Spiritual Maturity: 12 Golden Rules for Inner Transformation

"This book is a gentle yet powerful guide that awakened a deeper sense of purpose within me. Each golden rule felt like a mirror reflecting truths I needed to embrace. Shree Shambav's wisdom is timeless, poetic, and profoundly grounding. It's not just a read—it's a journey into the heart of who you truly are. A must-read for anyone seeking lasting peace, clarity, and inner transformation."

The Inner Battlefield: Overcoming the Enemies of the Mind and Soul:

"This book is a powerful revelation—an honest mirror to the battles we fight within. Every chapter is a step closer to clarity, peace, and emotional mastery. Shree Shambav brilliantly transforms ancient wisdom into practical guidance for modern souls. It awakened in me a new strength to face my fears and rise above inner turmoil. A must-read for anyone seeking true inner victory and lasting transformation."

The Seeker's Gold – Unlocking Life's Greatest Treasure

The Seeker's Gold is a soul-stirring masterpiece that goes far beyond the pursuit of wealth—it is a journey into the heart of what truly matters. Each chapter unfolds with poetic wisdom and emotional depth, revealing that life's real treasure is not found in riches but in the transformation of the self. As the protagonist evolves through trials, love, and profound realisations, so does the reader. This book is a mirror for every dreamer, a lantern for every seeker, and a companion for anyone walking the path of purpose. A timeless tale that stays with you long after the final page.

Born to Rise Series I & II:

Born to Rise – Series I & II is a profound awakening—a journey that begins in silence and leads you to the core of your true power.

Series I reshapes your understanding of success, showing that clarity is more valuable than applause, and authenticity more powerful than performance.

Series II takes you deeper, unlocking the mindset and inner strategy behind meaningful, lasting growth—not just in wealth, but in wisdom.

Together, these books are not just guides—they are soul mirrors, revealing the truths you've forgotten and the strength you've always held.

This is more than reading—it's remembering who you are, and rising with purpose, not pressure.

The Law of Attraction: A Soulful Path

The Law of Attraction: A Soulful Path is more than a guide—it's a spiritual companion. Shree Shambav has beautifully woven timeless wisdom with practical tools, helping me understand that manifestation isn't about control—it's about inner alignment and grace. Each rule in this book felt like a key unlocking something dormant within me. I've read many books on the Law of Attraction, but none touched my heart like this one. Through soulful rituals, deep reflection, and gentle encouragement, I began releasing old fears and stepping into clarity and peace. This book helped me move from desperation to trust, from wanting to becoming. It's a must-read for anyone yearning for meaning, healing, and true, lasting transformation.

Whispers of Stillness: Where the soul listens beyond the noise Series

Whispers of Stillness is a rare and luminous work that speaks softly yet transforms deeply. Each couplet feels like a breath of wisdom—gentle, precise, and profoundly awakening. Moving gracefully through Virtue, Wealth, and Love, the series invites quiet reflection, ethical clarity, and emotional truth. This is not poetry to rush through, but to live with. A timeless companion for seekers, leaders, and sensitive hearts, it restores stillness where the soul can truly listen.

Whispers of a Silent Monk

Whispers of a Silent Monk is a luminous blend of poetry, parable, and spiritual reflection. With rare grace and emotional depth, Shree Shambav invites us into a village transformed by silence, compassion, and timeless wisdom. Each chapter is a meditative journey into the heart's questions—of love, loss, identity, and liberation. This book doesn't just speak to the soul; it listens with it. A masterwork of gentle storytelling and profound insight, it reminds us that sometimes, the most powerful truths are whispered—not shouted. A must-read for seekers, dreamers, and those yearning for a deeper, quieter way of being.

"Mastering the Art of Gratitude:

A Journey from Acknowledgement to Awakening, Volume One" is a luminous guide for those seeking to transform gratitude from a mere emotion into a living state of awareness. Shree Shambav beautifully blends spiritual insight, psychological depth, and poetic reflection to awaken the reader's inner grace. This book reminds us that gratitude is not learned — it is remembered, rediscovered, and lived moment by moment, until appreciation becomes our natural rhythm of being.

The Power of Manifestation

"The Power of Manifestation is more than just a book—it's an awakening. Shree Shambav beautifully weaves ancient wisdom with modern science, offering not just theories but a practical guide for anyone yearning to turn their inner visions into lived reality. This book reminds us that manifestation is not wishful thinking, but a sacred, conscious collaboration with the universe. If you've ever felt the quiet ache for a life aligned with your heart's deepest desires—this book is your map."

ACKNOWLEDGEMENTS

To my grandfathers, grandmothers, mothers, fathers, aunts, uncles, neighbours, sisters, brothers, friends, and teachers, they poured in endless moral stories, retellings of Ramayana, Mahabharata, Puranas, Upanishads, and so on.

My teachers, neighbours, and kindred souls. Who provided us with a stage to perform wonderful Puranic stories and were gracious enough to acknowledge our efforts.

The artists and translators of epics have served as a source of inspiration, invigorating our spirits, making these works accessible, and enabling us to grasp the profound depths and deeper dimensions they contain.

I also cherish the stimulating conversations; I had with my wonderful mothers, Punitha Muniswamy and Uma Devi.

Our family's youngest member, Aadhya, who always overwhelmed me with questions, inspired this book.

I would likewise prefer to express gratitude to Mr Sivakumar, Mrs Roopa Sivakumar, Mr Akshaya

Rajesh, Ms Akshatha Rajesh, Ms Apeksha Prabhu, Mr Akanksh Prabhu, Mr Nikash Sarasambi, and Mrs Spoorthi Nikash for their valuable inputs.

I must thank Mr Rajesh, Mr Savan Prabhu, Mrs Revathi Rajesh, Mrs Rajani Sarasambi, and Mrs Manju Reshma, who encouraged me and often suggested writing a book. Their unwavering belief that I had something valuable to offer kept me going during my writing sessions.

Love you all,

Shree Shambav

Web: www.shambav.org

Email: shreeshambav@gmail.com

9 789356 920545

Printed at Repro India Ltd.